H. Hoover

D0509216

# KNITS FOR
# Kids & Teddies
## TOO

# KNITS FOR
# Kids & Teddies
## TOO

*The seed of creation for this book was to design original children's and bears' wear to be knitted in the natural fibres of pure new wool or cotton.*

CLICK CLACK
Cleckheaton

BayBooks
An imprint of HarperCollins*Publishers*

# Contents

# Introduction

## Sizes and Measurements

Each pattern has a tabled list of measurements for easy reference. Make sure you measure your child before starting to knit. Note: Figures in brackets throughout the pattern refer to the larger sizes. Where only one number appears it applies to all sizes. If you are knitting a complicated pattern you may find it helpful to mark the directions for the size you are knitting with a highlighting pen.

## Knitting Needles

Metric sizes are referred to throughout the pattern. Needles are available in different lengths. Always consider the size of the garment you are knitting before purchasing needles. Needles that are too short for the number of stitches required will make knitting difficult.

When knitting with a set of 4 double pointed needles, divide stitches equally over 3 needles and use remaining needle to knit stitches. Each needle is used in turn to knit off. If working with a large number of stitches, corks on the ends of each needle will prevent stitches being pushed off.

## Tension

Each pattern has a tension guide. It is most important that you knit a tension square before starting any pattern, otherwise the measurements will be wrong and the finished garment may differ in appearance from the garment photographed. Tension for plain and textured patterns sometimes differs and it is necessary to knit two squares. If your square is smaller than specified you will need to use larger size needles. If your square is larger you will need to use thinner needles.

## Abbreviations

cm = centimetres
mm = millimetres
pr = pair
st/s = stitch/es
K = knit
P = purl
st st = stocking stitch (1 row K, 1 row P)
beg = beginning
inc = increase
dec = decrease
patt = pattern
foll = following
as folls = as follows
rep = repeat
rem = remaining
rib = (K1, P1) rep until end of row or for number of sts indicated
cont = continued
alt = alternate
tog = together
MC = main colour
C1 = first contrast colour
C2 = second contrast colour
C3 = third contrast colour, etc.
yfwd = yarn forward
yrn = yarn round needle
M1 = Pick up loop which lies before next stitch, place on left-hand needle and knit through back of loop.
tbl = through back of loop
ybk = yarn back
sl1 = slip one stitch: insert the right-hand needle into the next stitch on the left-hand needle as if to knit it. Slip the stitch off the needle onto the right-hand needle.
psso = pass the slipped stitch over: with the point of the left-hand needle, lift up the slipped stitch and pass it over the stitch just knitted and off the needle.

*Notes for Beginners*

The following instructions will help you with some of the basic skills and stitches needed to successfully complete the patterns in this book.

BASIC STITCHES

Knit stitch and purl stitch are the two basic knitting stitches. When every row is knitted back and forth on two needles, garter stitch is formed. When one row is knitted and next purled, stocking stitch is formed. When working in the round, knitting every row produces stocking stitch. A combination of knit and purl stitches, usually one knit stitch and one purl stitch, in the same row, is known as ribbing. Ribbing is used on sleeve and body edges to form a neat, stretchable finish. It is usually worked on smaller needles than the body of the garment.

KNIT STITCH

1. With the yarn at the back, insert your right-hand needle from front to back into the 1st stitch on your left-hand needle.

2. Bring your working yarn under and over the point of your right-hand needle.

3. Draw a loop through and slide the 1st stitch off your left-hand needle while the new stitch is retained on your right-hand needle. Continue in this way to the end of the row.

4. To knit the next row, turn the work around so that the back is facing you and the worked stitches are held on the needle in your left hand. Proceed to make stitches as given above, with initially empty needle held in your right hand.

PURL STITCH

1. With the yarn at the front, insert your right-hand needle from back to front into the 1st stitch on your left-hand needle.

2. Bring your working yarn over and around the point of your right-hand needle.

3. Draw a loop through and slide the 1st stitch off your left-hand needle while the new stitch is retained on your right-hand needle. Continue in this way to the end of the row.

4. To purl the next row, turn the work around so that the back is facing you and the worked stitches are held on the needle in your left hand. Proceed to make stitches as given above, with the initially empty needle held in your right hand.

INCREASING

YARN FORWARD

This method is used to make a stitch between two knit stitches. After the 1st knit stitch the yarn is at the back of the work. Bring the yarn forward between the needles. Knit the next stitch as usual.

YARN ROUND NEEDLE

1. This is used to make a stitch between 2 purl stitches. After the 1st purl stitch the yarn is at the front of the work. Take the yarn over then under the right-hand needle. Purl the next stitch as usual. 2. The same method is used to make a stitch between a knit and a purl stitch. After the knit stitch take the yarn under, over, then under the right-hand needle. Purl the next stitch as usual.

YARN BACK

This method is used to make a stitch between a purl and knit stitch. After the purl stitch the yarn is at the front of the work. Take yarn back over the right-hand needle. Knit the next stitch as usual.

MAKE 1

Pick up loop which lies before next stitch, place on left-hand needle and knit through back of loop.

DECREASING

KNIT 2 STITCHES TOGETHER (K2 TOG)

1. Insert the right-hand needle knitwise in the 2nd and then the 1st stitch on the left-hand needle. Take the yarn under and over the point of the right-hand needle.

2. Draw the yearn through the 1st and 2nd stitches on the left-hand needle, discarding both stitches at the same time, thus ending with 1 stitch only.

PURL 2 STITCHES TOGETHER (P2 TOG)

1. Insert the right-hand needle purlwise into the 1st and then the 2nd stitch on the left-hand needle. Take the yarn over and under the point of the right-hand needle.

2. Draw the yarn through the 1st and 2nd stitches on the left-hand needle, discarding both stitches at the same time, thus ending with 1 stitch only.

SLIP 1, KNIT 1, PASS SLIPPED STITCH OVER (SL1, K1, PSSO)

1. Insert the right-hand needle into the next stitch on the left-hand needle as if to knit it. Slip the stitch off the needle onto the right-hand needle.

2. Knit the next stitch on the left-hand needle as usual. With the point of the left-hand needle, lift up the slipped stitch and pass it over the stitch just knitted and off the needle.

## CASTING OFF

When you end a piece of knitting, such as a sleeve, or part of a piece of knitting, such as up to the neck, you must secure all the stitches by 'casting off'. This is preferably done on a knit row but you can employ the same technique on a purl or a rib row.

### IN KNIT STITCH

1. Knit the first 2 stitches and insert the top of your left-hand needle through the 1st stitch.
2. Lift the 1st stitch over the 2nd stitch and discard it. Knit the next stitch and continue to lift the 1st stitch over the 2nd stitch to the end of the row. For the last stitch, cut your yarn, slip the end through the stitch and pull the yarn to fasten.

### IN PURL STITCH

Purl the first 2 (and all subsequent) stitches and continue as for knit stitch above.

### IN RIB STITCH

Knit or purl the first 2 (and all subsequent) stitches as they appear and continue as for knit stitch above.

## PART KNITTING OR INTARSIA KNITTING (CHANGING COLOURS)

### WORKING A KNIT ROW

Keep the yarns at the back of the work throughout and repeat the following for each new colour. Knit across the stitches in the 1st colour. Take this end of yarn over the top of the next colour to be used and drop it. Pick up the next colour under this strand of yarn and take it over the strand ready to knit the next stitch.

### WORKING A PURL ROW

Keep the yarns at the front of the work throughout and repeat the following for each new colour. Purl across the stitches in the 1st colour. Take this end of yarn over the top of the next colour to be used and drop it. Pick up the next colour under this strand of yarn and take it over the strand ready to purl the next stitch. When working with small sections of colour in the centre of a graph, try using bobbins. Wind a quantity of yarn around the bobbin and place the end of the yarn through the slot to hold it. Unwind only enough yarn to knit the required stitches, then place the yarn in the slot, keeping the bobbin close to the work.

## READING THE GRAPHS

Except where otherwise indicated, when working from graphs, read even-numbered rows (purl rows) from left to right and odd-numbered rows (knit rows) from right to left — 1 square equals one stitch.
Colour changes are indicated with a code to denote the colours. When working with a number of colours, you may find it easier to colour in the chart with the shades you intend to use before beginning to knit. It may also be helpful to first enlarge the graphs on a photocopier.

## PICKING UP STITCHES

1. Stitches often need to be picked up round neck edges and armholes so that a neckband and armhole band can be knitted. To ensure they are picked up evenly, divide the edge into equal sections and mark them with pins.
2. Divide the number of sections into the number of stitches specified in the pattern and start picking up an equal number of stitches per section. Insert the top of the needle into a row end on vertical edges or a stitch on horizontal edges.
3. With the yarn at the back of the work, take it under and over the point of the needle, and draw a loop through.
4. Insert the tip of the needle into the next stitch or row end. Take the yarn under and over the point of the needle and draw a loop through.
Carry on in this way until the correct number of stitches have been picked up.

# Stitch glossary

## Knitting Stitch Embroidery

Knitting Stitch embroidery is particularly effective on plain knitting (stocking stitch). Your garment can be quickly transformed by the addition of embroidered motifs to yoke or pockets. Children love to have an illustration from their favourite books transferred to a cardigan or jumper.

Use the same ply wool for embroidery as used in the garment. You could use a slightly thicker yarn if necessary, but a thinner yarn will not give a good result.

Knitting Stitch is worked directly over each knitted stitch, with a contrasting colour to represent the same knitted stitch, as before. Each square on the graph represents one stitch. Insert the needle from back of work into the centre of the knitted stitch and draw through. *Insert needle from right to left, underneath the two loops of the same stitch one row above and draw through. Then insert needle back into original place where needle was first inserted, draw underneath the two loops still working from right to left, and out into the centre of the next stitch (thus completing one knitting stitch). Rep from * to end of graph pattern.

Odd numbered rows (knit rows) of pattern are worked from right to left and even numbered rows (purl rows) from left to right, until the motifs have been completed.

## Stem Stitch

This is a widely used stitch as it is complementary to Satin Stitch and other filling stitches and is good for outlining and making curving lines. Working from left to right, pass the needle to the left under two or three threads of the fabric. Move along the line of the design to the right and make a second stitch to the left, picking up the same number of threads. The needle always emerges just above the previous stitch, giving the effect of a fine twisted cord.

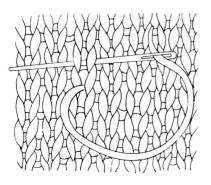

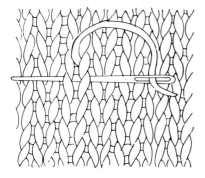

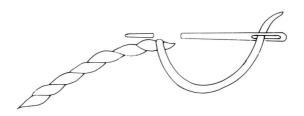

## Bullion Stitch

Make a back stitch, the size of the Bullion Stitch required, and bring the needle point out where it first emerged, without pulling right through. Wind the thread round the needle point as many times as required. Holding the left thumb on the coiled thread, pull the needle through. Still holding the coiled thread, turn the needle back to where it was inserted and insert in the same place. Pull the needle through.

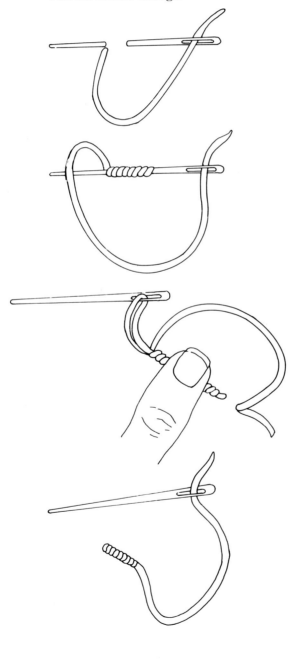

## These instructions explain how to cast on for Guernsey Edge

Using 3 balls of yarn, proceed as follows:
1. Take one ball of yarn and make a slip knot on needle. Holding ends of rem 2 balls (short ends upwards) in left hand, wind short ends twice anti-clockwise around thumb of left hand. Holding needle with slip knot in right hand, insert needle from bottom to top under the 4 strands on thumb.
2. Using the yarn attached to the slip knot, knit one stitch in usual manner and slip the four strands from thumb. Pull the double yarn firmly to the needle to form a knot.
3. Yarn forward: bring yarn under needle, then over into knitting position again, thus making a st.
4. Wind double yarn twice anti-clockwise around the left thumb. Knit one stitch through double yarn and slip four strands off as before, pulling double yarn firmly to needle to make a knot. 4 sts on needle. Rep steps 3 and 4 until there is one st less than required number, then rep step 4 again: odd number of sts. Break off double yarn, turn and proceed as instructed in patt.

## Thumb Method

This method requires only one needle and is used for a very elastic edge or when the rows immediately after the cast-on stitches are worked in garter stitch (every row knitted). The length of yarn between the cut end and the slip knot is used for making the stitches. You will learn to assess this length by eye, according to the number of stitches required, but as a general rule the length of yarn from the slip knot to the end of the yarn should be about 3 or 4 times the required finished width.
1. Make a slip knot the required length from the end of the yarn (for a practice piece make this length about 1m). Place the slip knot on a needle and hold the needle in the right hand with the ball end of yarn over your first finger. Hold the other end in the palm of your left hand. *Wind the loose end of the yarn around the left thumb from front to back.
2. Insert the needle upwards through the yarn on the thumb.
3. Take the yarn over the point of the needle with your right index finger.

# KNITTING NEEDLE SUGGESTED EQUIVALENT CHART

| Canadian & UK Sizes | 000 | 00 | 0 | 1 | 2 | 3 | 4 | 5 | 6 | 7 | 8 | 9 | - | 10 | 11 | 12 | 13 |
|---|---|---|---|---|---|---|---|---|---|---|---|---|---|---|---|---|---|
| Metric Sizes | | 10 | 9 | 8 | 7½ | 7 | 6½ | 6 | 5½ | 5 | 4½ | 4 | 3¾ | 3½ | 3¼ | 3 | 2¾ | 2¼ |
| US Sizes | | 15 | 13 | 11 | - | - | 10½ | 10 | 9 | 8 | 7 | 6 | 5 | 4 | 3 | - | 2 | 1 |

4. Draw the yarn back through the loop on the thumb to form a stitch.

5. Remove the yarn from your left thumb and pull the loose end to tighten the stitch. Repeat from the *until the required number of stitches has been cast on.

## Blanket Stitch

This stitch may be used along an edge where there is no ribbing.

## Tassels

Tassels are often used to decorate hats and novelty items, and can also be attached to the ends of a twisted cord.

1. Cut a rectangle of card as wide as the required length of the finished tassel. Wind the yarn around the card until the required thickness is reached. Break the yarn, thread through a sewing needle and pass the needle under all the loops. Do not remove the needle.

2. Tie the end of the yarn firmly around the loops, remove the card and cut through the loops, at the opposite end to the knot.

3. Wind the end of yarn around all the loops below the fold and fasten securely. Pass the needle through the top and use the end to sew in place. Trim the ends neatly.

## Daisy Stitch

This is a method of working individual chain stitches to form 'petals' which can be grouped together to make a 'flower' of 4, 5 or more petals.

## AMERICAN KNITTERS PLEASE NOTE:

*The American equivalents of Australian terminologies are as follows:*

| AUSTRALIAN | AMERICAN |
|---|---|
| yfwd | yarn over (yo) |
| yrn | yarn over (yo) |
| tension | gauge |
| cast off | bind off |

# Teddy Bear's
# Picnic

# *Tunic &*
# *cloche hat*

**TENSION**
*These garments have been designed at a tension of 22 sts and 30 rows to 10cm over stocking st, using 4.00mm needles.*

## *Measurements*
Years

| 1 | 2 | 3 | 4 | 6 |
|---|---|---|---|---|

Tunic

To fit chest (cm):

| 52.5 | 55 | 57.5 | 60 | 65 |
|---|---|---|---|---|

Actual measurement (cm):

| 60 | 64 | 67 | 70 | 77 |
|---|---|---|---|---|

Length (cm):

| 36 | 38 | 40 | 42 | 46cm |
|---|---|---|---|---|

Sleeve length (cm):

| 21 | 23 | 25 | 28 | 33 |
|---|---|---|---|---|

Hat

To fit around head (approx) (cm):

| 49 | 51 | 51 | 52 | 52 |
|---|---|---|---|---|

Length (approx) (cm):

| 13 | 14 | 15 | 15 | 16 |
|---|---|---|---|---|

## *Materials*
Cleckheaton Country 8ply or Country Naturals 8 ply or Cleckheaton Machinewash 8 ply or Cleckheaton 8 ply Pure Wool (50g balls)

Tunic

| 6 | 7 | 7 | 8 | 9 |
|---|---|---|---|---|

Hat

| 1 | 1 | 1 | 1 | 1 |
|---|---|---|---|---|

One pair each 3.25mm and 4.00mm knitting needles for Tunic and one set of 4.00mm knitting needles for Hat or the required size to give correct tension; one spare 4.00mm knitting needle and a piece of cardboard 12cm x 8cm for making tassel for Tunic; knitter's needle for sewing seams and finishing; Sizes 1, 2 and 3 for

Tunic only - 3.50mm crochet hook and 3 buttons for shoulder opening.

## TUNIC
### *Back*
Using 4.00mm needles, cast on 69 (73-75-79-87) sts using thumb method.

**NOTE:** We have used the thumb method (see Stitch Glossary) for casting on sts as this gives a neater edge to this particular design.

**1ST ROW:** Purl.
**2ND ROW:** Knit.
**3RD ROW:** K5 (2-3-5-4), * yfwd, K3, sl1, K2tog, psso, K3, yfwd, K1, rep from * to last 4 (1-2-4-3) st/s, K4 (1-2-4-3).
**4TH AND ALT ROWS:** Purl.
**5TH ROW:** K5 (2-3-5-4), * K1, yfwd, K2, sl1, K2tog, psso, K2, yfwd, K2, rep from * to last 4 (1-2-4-3) st/s, K4 (1-2-4-3).
**7TH ROW:** K5 (2-3-5-4), * K2, yfwd, K1, sl1, K2tog, psso, K1, yfwd, K3, rep from * to last 4 (1-2-4-3) st/s, K4 (1-2-4-3).
**9TH ROW:** K5 (2-3-5-4), * K3, yfwd, sl1, K2tog, psso, yfwd, K4, rep from * to last 4 (1-2-4-3) st/s, K4 (1-2-4-3).
**10TH ROW:** Purl.
Work in stocking st until work measures 22 (23-24-25-27) cm from deepest point of scallops, ending with a purl row.
Tie a marker at each end of last row to mark beg of armholes as there is no armhole shaping. **
Work a further 42 (44-48-50-56) rows stocking st.

## SHAPE SHOULDERS

Cast off 7 (8-8-8-9) sts at beg of next 4 rows, then 8 (7-7-8-9) sts at beg of foll 2 rows.

Cast off rem 25 (27-29-31-33) sts loosely.

## Yoke insert

Using 4.00mm needles, cast on 11 sts.

**1ST ROW:** K1, yfwd, K3, sl1, K2tog, psso, K3, yfwd, K1.

**2ND AND ALT ROWS:** Purl.

**3RD ROW:** K2, yfwd, K2, sl1, K2tog, psso, K2, yfwd, K2.

**5TH ROW:** K3, yfwd, K1, sl1, K2tog, psso, K1, yfwd, K3.

**7TH ROW:** K4, yfwd, sl1, K2tog, psso, yfwd, K4.

**9TH ROW:** Cast on 10 sts, (K1, yfwd, K3, sl1, K2tog, psso, K3, yfwd) across these 10 sts, K11, do not turn work.

\*\*\* With another ball of yarn cast on 10 sts to empty needle, then using needle holding work and attached yarn (yfwd, K3, sl1, K2tog, psso, K3, yfwd, K1) across these 10 sts, working first st firmly. Cut off extra ball. 31 sts.

**11TH ROW:** K2, * yfwd, K2, sl1, K2tog, psso, K2, yfwd *, K13, rep from * to * once, K2.

**13TH ROW:** K3, * yfwd, K1, sl1, K2tog, psso, K1, yfwd *, K15, rep from * to * once, K3.

**15TH ROW:** K4, * yfwd, sl1, K2tog, psso, yfwd *, K17, rep from * to * once, K4.

along scalloped edge, knitting up 7 sts evenly along each side of scallop and 9 sts evenly along cast-on edge of each scallop, thus ending with 7 sts knitted up evenly along side of other end scallop.

**NEXT ROW:** Knit.
**NEXT ROW:** Purl.
**NEXT ROW:** Knit.
Cast off purlways.

## Front

Work as given for Back to **
Work a further 18 (18-20-20-22) rows stocking st.

### PLACE YOKE INSERT
**NEXT ROW:** K9 (11-12-14-18), holding needle with Yoke Insert sts in front of Front piece so that wrong side of insert is against right side of front, (knit one st from insert and one st from Front tog) 51 times, K9 (11-12-14-18). 69 (73-75-79-87) sts.
Work 11 (11-13-13-15) rows stocking st, beg with a purl row.

### SHAPE NECK
**NEXT ROW:** K29 (31-31-33-37), cast off next 11 (11-13-13-13) sts loosely, knit to end.
Cont on last 29 (31-31-33-37) sts and dec one st at neck edge in every row until 25 (27-27-29-33) sts rem, then in alt rows until 22 (23-23-24-27) sts rem.
Work 2 rows.

### SHAPE SHOULDER
Cast off 7 (8-8-8-9) sts at beg of next row and foll alt row.
Work 1 row. Cast off rem 8 (7-7-8-9) sts.
With wrong side facing, join yarn to rem 29 (31-31-33-37) sts and dec one st at neck edge in every row until 25 (27-27-29-33) sts rem, then in alt rows until 22 (23-23-24-27) sts rem.
Work 1 row.

### SHAPE SHOULDER
Cast off 7 (8-8-8-9) sts at beg of next row and foll alt row.
Work 1 row. Cast off rem 8 (7-7-8-9) sts.

## Sleeves

Using 3.25mm needles, cast on 33 (35-37-39-39) sts.

**17TH ROW:** Cast on 10 sts, (K1, yfwd, K3, sl1, K2tog, psso, K3, yfwd) across these 10 sts, K31, do not turn work. Complete as for 9th rows from ***. 51 sts.
**19TH ROW:** As 11th row, working K33 instead of K13 in centre.
**21ST ROW:** As 13th row, working K35 instead of K15 in centre.
**23RD ROW:** As 15th row, working K37 instead of K17 in centre.
**24TH ROW:** Purl.
Leave sts on spare needle.

### EDGING
With right side of Yoke Insert facing, using 4.00mm needles and working first down side of end scallop, knit up 87 sts evenly

*Cardigan with ruffle edge & matching teddy's hat (page 20); ABC jumper (page 31); Teddy's striped jacket (page 29); Fair Isle cardigan & beret (page 25); Lace collars (page 19); and Tunic & cloche hat (page 14).*

*Rug from Linen and Lace of Balmain. Tea set from Julia Walton. Blouse, cream and pink skivvies, skirt, pinafore and denim shoes from Osh Kosh B'Gosh. Purple skivvy, leggings, rose and bandana from Homegrown. Brooches from Hide 'n Seek and The Teddy Bear Shop. Teddies from The Teddy Bear Shop and Teddy & Friends. Other shoes from Shoes & Sox.*

**1st Row:** K2, * P1, K1, rep from * to last st, K1.

**2nd Row:** K1, * P1, K1, rep from * to end. Rep 1st and 2nd rows 4 (4-5-5-7) times, then 1st row once.

**Next Row:** Rib 0 (2-4-6-2), * inc in next st, rib 3 (3-2-2-2), rep from * to last 1 (1-3-3-1) st/s, rib 1 (1-3-3-1). 41 (43-47-49-51) sts [12 (12-14-14-18) rows rib in all].
Change to 4.00mm needles.
Work 4 rows stocking st.

**Next Row:** K2, * M1, knit to last 2 sts, M1, K2.

Cont in stocking st, inc one st (as before) at each end of foll alt (alt-alt-4th-4th) rows until there are 49 (49-53-73-81) sts, then in foll 4th (4th-4th-6th-6th) rows until there are 65 (69-75-77-85) sts.

Cont (without further inc) until work measures 21 (23-25-28-33) cm from beg, ending with a purl row.

**Shape Top**
Cast off 5 (5-6-6-7) sts at beg of next 8 rows, then 6 (7-6-6-6) sts at beg of foll 2 rows.
Cast off rem 13 (15-15-17-17) sts.

## Neck edging
Using 4.00mm needles, cast on 63 (73-73-83-83) sts, using thumb method.
Work rows 1 to 10 incl of Lower Edging Patt of Back as for 2nd size.
Cast off loosely.

## To make up
Join right shoulder seam. Sew Neck Edging evenly in position. Join left shoulder and neck edging seam. Sizes 1, 2 and 3 only: join for 3cm only from armhole edge to allow for shoulder opening. With right side facing and using 3.50mm hook, work 1 row dc evenly around shoulder opening, working three 3ch buttonloops evenly along front shoulder. Sew buttons in position.

All sizes: sew in sleeves evenly between markers, placing centres of sleeves to shoulder seams. Join side and sleeve seams. Make a tassel (see Stitch Glossary)

8cm in length (finished) and sew in position to lower edge of yoke insert as illustrated.

# HAT

Using set of 4.00mm needles, cast on 80 (90-90-100-100) sts using thumb method.

**Begin Lower Edging**

**1st Round:** Purl.

**2nd Round:** Purl.

**3rd Round:** * K1, yfwd, K3, sl1, K2tog, psso, K3, yfwd, rep from * to end.

**4th and Alt Rounds:** Knit.

**5th Round:** * K2, yfwd, K2, sl1, K2tog, psso, K2, yfwd, K1, rep from * to end.

**7th Round:** * K3, yfwd, K1, sl1, K2tog, psso, K1, yfwd, K2, rep from * to end.

**9th Round:** * K4, yfwd, sl1, K2tog, psso, yfwd, K3, rep from * to end.

**10th Round:** Knit.

Rep last round until work measures 8 (8-9-9-9) cm from deepest point of scallops.

**Shape Crown**

**Next Round:** * K2 tog, K8, rep from * to end. 72 (81-81-90-90) sts.
Knit 1 (2-2-2-2) round/s.

**Next Round:** * K2tog, K7, rep from * to end. 64 (72-72-80-80) sts.
Knit 1 (2-2-2-2) round/s.

**Next Round:** * K2tog, K6, rep from * to end. 56 (63-63-70-70) sts.
Knit 1 (1-1-1-2) round/s.

**Next Round:** * K2tog, K5, rep from * to end. 48 (54-54-60-60) sts.
Knit 1 (1-1-1-2) round/s.

**Next Round:** * K2tog, K4, rep from * to end. 40 (45-45-50-50) sts.
Knit 1 round.

**Next Round:** * K2tog, K3, rep from * to end. 32 (36-36-40-40) sts.
Knit 1 round.

**Next Round:** * K2tog, K2, rep from * to end. 24 (27-27-30-30) sts.
Knit 1 round.

**Next Round:** * K2tog, K1, rep from * to end. 16 (18-18-20-20) sts.

Break off yarn, run end through rem sts, draw up and fasten off securely.

# Lace collars

*Measurements*
Girl's collar

| Years | 1-2 | 3-4 | 5-6 |
|---|---|---|---|
| To fit neck (cm): | 26 | 28 | 30 |
| Width (at deepest point)(cm): | | | |
| | 13 | 13 | 13 |

| Teddy's collar | Small | | Large |
|---|---|---|---|
| To fit neck (cm): | 23 | | 30 |
| Width (cm): | 7 | | 8 |

*Materials*
Cleckheaton Cotton Soft 8 ply (50g balls)

| | | |
|---|---|---|
| Girl's collar: | 1 | 2 |
| 2 | | |
| Teddy's collar | 1 | 1 |

One pair 3.75mm needles or the required size to give correct tension; a 3.00mm crochet hook; 1 small button.

## GIRL'S COLLAR

Using 3.75mm needles, cast on 26 sts.
**1st Row (wrong side):** Knit.
**2nd Row:** K5, P10, (K2tog, yfwd) twice, K3, (yfwd) twice, K2tog, (yfwd) twice, K2. 29 sts.
**3rd Row:** K2, (knit 1st yfwd, then purl 2nd yfwd, K1) twice, P6, K10, turn.
**4th Row:** K9, (K2tog, yfwd) twice, K11.
**5th Row:** K2, (yfwd) twice, K2tog, K1, K2tog, (yfwd) twice, K2tog, K1, P14, K5. 30 sts.
**6th Row:** K13, (K2tog, yfwd) twice, K1, (K3, knit 1st yfwd, then purl 2nd yfwd) twice, K2.
**7th Row:** K12, P13, turn.
**8th Row:** K10, (yfwd, K2tog) twice, K2, K2tog, (yfwd) twice, sl1, K2tog, psso, (yfwd) twice, (K2tog) twice. 29 sts.
**9th Row:** K2, (knit 1st yfwd, then purl 2nd yfwd, K1) twice, K2, P14, K5.

**10th Row:** K5, P11, yon, K2tog, yfwd, K2tog, K9.
**11th Row:** Cast off 3 sts knitways, K6 (incl st already on needle), P4, K11, turn.
**12th Row:** P12, yon, K2tog, yfwd, K2tog, K5. 26 sts.
**13th Row:** K5, P4, K17.
Rep rows 2 to 13 incl 15 (16-17) times, then rows 2 to 12 incl once. 17 (18-19) scallops in all.
Cast off loosely knitways.

## TEDDY'S COLLAR

Using 3.75mm needles, cast on 15 (18) sts.
**1st Row (wrong side):** Knit.
**2nd Row:** K9 (12), K2tog, yfwd, K1, K2tog, K1. 14 (17) sts.
**3rd Row:** K4, yfwd, K2tog, K2, yfwd, K2tog, K4 (7).
**4th Row:** K7 (10), K2tog, yfwd, K1, K2tog, K2. 13 (16) sts.
**5th Row:** K7, yfwd, K2tog, K1, turn.
**6th Row:** K5, yfwd, K2tog, K1, (yfwd) twice, K2. 15 (18) sts.
**7th Row:** K2, knit 1st yfwd, then purl 2nd yfwd, K2, yfwd, K3, yfwd, K2tog, K4 (7). 16 (19) sts.
**8th Row:** K10 (13), yfwd, K2tog, K4.
**9th Row:** Cast off 2 sts, K3, (incl st on right-hand needle), yfwd, K5, yfwd, K2tog, K1, turn.
**10th Row:** K6, K2tog, yfwd, K1, K2tog, K1. 14 (17) sts.
Rep rows 3 to 10 incl 18 (23) times. 19 (24) scallops in all.
Cast off loosely knitways.

## *To make up (either)*

Using crochet hook, work a 3ch buttonloop at neck edge of collar. Sew on button.

**Tension**
*This collar has been designed at a tension of 23 sts and 31 rows to 10cm over stocking st, using 3.75mm needles.*
**Note:** *When turning, take yarn under needle and onto other side of work, slip next st onto right-hand needle, take yarn under needle and back to original position, slip st back onto left-hand needle, then turn and proceed as instructed. This avoids holes in work.*

# Cardigan with ruffle edge

## & MATCHING TEDDY'S HAT

**TENSION**

*These garments have been designed at a tension of 22 sts and 30 rows to 10cm over stocking st, using 4.00mnm needles.*

**ABBREVIATIONS**

*S12 = Slip 2; p2sso = pass two slip sts over.*
**NOTE:** *Always slip sts knitways throughout patt.*

*Measurements*

Years

| 1 | 2 | 3 | 4 | 6 |
|---|---|---|---|---|

Cardigan
To fit chest (cm):

| 52.5 | 55 | 57.5 | 60 | 65 |
|---|---|---|---|---|

Actual measurement (approx) (cm):

| 60 | 64 | 67 | 70 | 77 |
|---|---|---|---|---|

Length (cm):

| 36 | 38 | 40 | 42 | 46 |
|---|---|---|---|---|

Sleeve length (cm):

| 19 | 21 | 23 | 26 | 31 |
|---|---|---|---|---|

Teddy's Hat
To fit head (cm):

| 32 | 48 |
|---|---|

Finished Length (approx) (cm):

| 8 | 10 |
|---|---|

*Materials*

Cleckheaton Country 8 ply or Country Naturals 8 ply (50g balls)
Cardigan

| 5 | 6 | 6 | 7 | 7 |
|---|---|---|---|---|

Hat

| 1 | 2 |
|---|---|

or Cleckheaton Machinewash 8 ply or Cleckheaton Pure Wool 8 ply (50g balls)
Cardigan

| 6 | 7 | 8 | 8 | 9 |
|---|---|---|---|---|

Hat

| 1 | 2 |
|---|---|

One pair each 3.25mm and 4.00mm knitting needles for Cardigan, one set of 4.00mm and one pair 4.00mm knitting needles for Hat, or the required size to give correct tension; 6 (7-7-7-7) buttons for Cardigan; piece of cardboard 6cm x 4cm for making Hat tassels; knitter's needle for sewing seams.

## CARDIGAN

### *Back*

Using 4.00mm needles, cast on 171 (175-191-195-215) sts to work ruffle.

**1ST ROW (WRONG SIDE):** K2 (4-2-4-4), * P7, K3, rep from * ending last rep with K2 (4-2-4-4) instead of K3.

**2ND ROW:** P2 (4-2-4-4), * K7, P3, rep from * ending last rep with P2 (4-2-4-4) instead of P3.

**3RD ROW:** As 1st row.

**4TH ROW:** P2 (4-2-4-4), * K2, sl2, K1, p2sso, K2, P3, rep from * ending last rep with P2 (4-2-4-4) instead of P3. 137 (141-153-157-173) sts.

**5TH ROW:** K2 (4-2-4-4), * P5, K3, rep from * ending last rep with K2 (4-2-4-4) instead of K3.

**6TH ROW:** P2 (4-2-4-4), * K5, P3, rep from * ending last rep with P2 (4-2-4-4) instead of P3.

**7TH ROW:** As 5th row.

**8TH ROW:** P2 (4-2-4-4), * K1, sl2, K1, p2sso, K1, P3, rep from * ending last rep with P2 (4-2-4-4) instead of P3. 103 (107-115-119-131) sts.

**9TH ROW:** K2 (4-2-4-4), * P3, K3, rep from * ending last rep with K2 (4-2-4-4) instead of K3.

**10TH ROW:** P2 (4-2-4-4), * K3, P3, rep from * ending last rep with P2 (4-2-4-4) instead of K3.

**11TH ROW:** As 9th row.

**12TH ROW:** P2 (4-2-4-4), * sl2, K1, p2sso, P3, rep from * ending last rep with P2 (4-2-4-4) instead of P3. 69 (73-77-81-89) sts.

**13TH ROW:** K2 (4-2-4-4), * P1, K3, rep from * ending last rep with K2 (4-2-4-4) instead of K3.

**14TH ROW:** P2 (4-2-4-4), * K1, P3, rep from * ending last rep with P2 (4-2-4-4) instead of P3.

** Work 2 rows stocking st, beg with a purl row.
Knit 1 row (wrong side).
Work 2 rows stocking st. **

BEGIN LACE BORDER

**1ST ROW (RIGHT SIDE):** K3 (1-3-1-1), * K1, yfwd, K3, slip 3rd st on right-hand needle over first 2 sts, rep from * to last 2 (0-2-0-0) sts, K2 (0-2-0-0).

**2ND AND ALT ROWS:** Purl.

**3RD ROW:** Knit.

**5TH ROW:** K2 (4-6-8-4), * yfwd, sl1, K1, psso, K6, rep from * ending last rep with K1 (3-5-7-3) instead of K6.

**7TH ROW:** K1 (3-5-1-3), (yfwd, sl1, K1, psso) 2 (2-2-1-2) time/s, K4, * (yfwd, sl1, K1, psso) twice, K4, rep from * to last 4 (6-8-2-6) sts, (yfwd, sl1, K1, psso) 2 (2-2-1-2) time/s, K0 (2-4-0-2).

**9TH ROW:** K2 (2-4-2-2), (yfwd, sl1, K1, psso) 2 (3-3-1-3) time/s, K2, * (yfwd, sl1, K1, psso) 3 times, K2, rep from * to last 5 (7-9-3-7) sts, (yfwd, sl1, K1, psso) 2 (3-3-1-3) time/s, K1 (1-3-1-1).

**11TH ROW:** As 7th row.

**13TH ROW:** As 5th row.

**15TH ROW:** Knit.

**17TH ROW:** As 1st row.

**18TH ROW:** Purl.

Last 18 rows form Lace Border.

BEGIN MAIN PATTERN

Work 4 rows stocking st.

**5TH ROW:** K6 (0-2-4-0), * P1, K7, rep from * to last 7 (1-3-5-1) st/s, P1, K6 (0-2-4-0).
Work 5 rows stocking st, beg with a purl row.

**11TH ROW:** K2 (4-6-0-4), * P1, K7, rep from * to last 3 (5-7-1-5) st/s, P1, K2 (4-6-0-4).

**12TH ROW:** Purl.

Last 12 rows form Main Patt for rem. Cont in Main Patt until work measures 35 (37-39-41-45) cm from beg, ending with a purl row.

SHAPE SHOULDERS

Keeping Main Patt correct, cast off 7 (8-8-9-10) sts at beg of next 4 rows, then 8 (7-9-8-10) sts at beg of foll 2 rows.
Cast off rem 25 (27-27-29-29) sts.

## Left front

Using 4.00mm needles, cast on 82 (84-92-94-104) sts to work ruffle.

**1ST ROW (WRONG SIDE):** * K3, P7, rep from * to last 2 (4-2-4-4) sts, K2 (4-2-4-4).

**2ND ROW:** P2 (4-2-4-4), * K7, P3, rep from * to end.

**3RD ROW:** As 1st row.

**4TH ROW:** P2 (4-2-4-4), * K2, sl2, K1, p2sso, K2, P3, rep from * to end. 66 (68-74-76-84) sts.

Keeping ruffle correct as given for Back as placed in last 4 rows, working a further 10 rows patt, thus completing ruffle, noting that there will be 50 (52-56-58-64) sts after 8th row and 34 (36-38-40-44) sts after 12th row.
Work as given for Back from ** to **.

BEGIN LACE BORDER

**1ST ROW (RIGHT SIDE):** K3 (1-3-1-1), * K1, yfwd, K3, slip 3rd st on right-hand needle over first 2 sts, rep from * to last 3 sts, K3.

**2ND AND ALT ROWS:** Purl.

**3RD ROW:** Knit.

**5TH ROW:** K2 (4-6-8-4), * yfwd, sl1, K1, psso, K6, rep from * to end.

**7TH ROW:** K1 (3-5-1-3), (yfwd, sl1, K1, psso) 2 (2-2-1-2) time/s, K4, * (yfwd, sl1, K1, psso) twice, K4, rep from * to last st, K1.

**9TH ROW:** K2 (2-4-2-2), (yfwd, sl1, K1, psso) 2 (3-3-1-3) time/s, K2, * (yfwd, sl1, K1, psso) 3 times, K2, rep from * to last 2 sts, K2.

Keeping Lace Border correct as for Back as placed in last 9 rows, work a further 9 rows patt, thus completing lace border.

### BEGIN MAIN PATTERN

Work 4 rows stocking st.

**5TH ROW:** K6 (0-2-4-0), * P1, K7, rep from * to last 4 sts, P1, K3.

Work 5 rows stocking st, beg with a purl row.

**11TH ROW:** K2 (4-6-0-4), * P1, K7, rep from * to end.

**12TH ROW:** Purl.

Last 12 rows for Main Patt for rem.

Cont in Main Patt until there are 11 (13-13-15-15) rows less than Back to beg of shoulder shaping, thus working last row on right side.

### SHAPE NECK

Cast off 5 (5-5-6-6) sts, patt to end. 29 (31-33-34-38) sts.

Keeping Main Patt correct, dec one st at neck edge in every row until 24 (26-28-31-35) sts rem, then in alt rows until 22 (23-25-26-30) sts rem.

Work 1 row.

### SHAPE SHOULDER

Cast off 7 (8-8-9-10) sts at beg of next row and foll alt row.

Work 1 row. Cast off rem 8 (7-9-8-10) sts.

## Right front

Using 4.00mm needles, cast on 82 (84-92-94-104) sts to work ruffle.

**1ST ROW (WRONG SIDE):** K2 (4-2-4-4), * P7, K3, rep from * to end.

**2ND ROW:** * P3, K7, rep from * to last 2 (4-2-4-4) sts, P2 (4-2-4-4).

**3RD ROW:** As 1st row.

**4TH ROW:** * P3, K2, sl2, K1, p2sso, K2, rep from * to last 2 (4-2-4-4) sts, P2 (4-2-4-4). 66 (68-74-76-84) sts.

Keeping ruffle correct as given for Back as placed in last 4 rows, work a further 10 rows patt thus completing ruffle, noting that there will be 50 (52-56-58-64) sts after 8th row and 34 (36-38-40-44) sts after 12th row.

Work as given for Back from ** to **.

### BEGIN LACE BORDER

**1ST ROW (RIGHT SIDE):** * K1, yfwd, K3, slip 3rd st on right-hand needle over first 2 sts, rep from * to last 2 (0-2-0-0) sts, K2 (0-2-0-0).

**2ND AND ALT ROWS:** Purl.

**3RD ROW:** Knit.

**5TH ROW:** K7, * yfwd, sl1, K1, psso, K6, rep from * ending last rep with K1 (3-5-7-3) instead of K6.

**7TH ROW:** K6, * (yfwd, sl1, K1, psso) twice, K4, rep from * to last 4 (6-8-2-6) sts, (yfwd, sl1, K1, psso) 2 (2-2-1-2) time/s, K0 (2-4-0-2).

**9TH ROW:** K5, * (yfwd, sl1, K1, psso) 3 times, K2, rep from * to last 5 (7-9-3-7) sts, (yfwd, sl1, K1, psso) 2 (3-3-1-3) time/s, K1 (1-3-1-1).
Keeping Lace Border correct as for Back as placed in last 9 rows, work a further 9 rows patt, thus completing lace border.

BEGIN MAIN PATTERN
Work 4 rows stocking st.
**5TH ROW:** K3, * P1, K7, rep from * to last 7 (1-3-5-1) st/s, P1, K6 (0-2-4-0).
Work 5 rows stocking st, beg with a purl row.
**11TH ROW:** * K7, P1, rep from * to last 2 (4-6-0-4) sts, K2 (4-6-0-4).
**12TH ROW:** Purl.
Last 12 rows form Main Patt for rem.
Cont in Main Patt until there are 12 (14-14-16-16) rows less than Back to beg of shoulder shaping, thus ending with a purl row.

SHAPE NECK
Cast off 5 (5-5-6-6) sts, patt to end. 29 (31-33-34-38) sts.
Work 1 row.
Keeping Main Patt correct, dec one st at neck edge in every row until 24 (26-28-31-35) sts rem, then in alt rows until 22 (23-25-26-30) sts rem.
Work 2 rows.

SHAPE SHOULDER
Cast off 7 (8-8-9-10) sts at beg of next row and foll alt row.
Work 1 row. Cast off rem 8 (7-9-8-10) sts.

## Sleeves
Using 4.00mm needles, cast on 91 (95-95-95-111) sts to work ruffle.
Work 14 rows of ruffle patt as for Sizes 1 (2-2-2-1) of Back, noting that there will be 73 (77-77-77-89) sts after 4th row, 55 (59-59-59-67) sts after 8th row and 37 (41-41-41-45) sts after 12th row.
Work as given for Back from ** to **, inc one st at each end of 2nd row and foll alt row and inc 4 sts evenly across last row. 45 (49-49-49-53) sts.

BEGIN MAIN PATTERN
Work 4 rows stocking st, inc one st at each

end of first row and foll alt (3rd-alt-3rd-3rd) row. 49 (53-53-53-57) sts.
**5TH ROW:** K0 (2-2-2-4), * P1, K7, rep from * to last 1 (3-3-3-5) st/s, P1, K0 (2-2-2-4).
Keeping Main Patt correct as given for Back as placed in last 5 rows (noting inc, and that 12 rows form patt) and noting to work extra sts into Main Patt, inc one st at each end of 1st (2nd-1st-2nd-2nd) row and foll 3rd rows until there are 65 (59-77-71-63) sts. Sizes 2, 4 and 6 only: then in foll 4th rows until there are (69-79-87) sts.
All sizes: cont in Main Patt (without further inc) until work measures 19 (21-23-26-31) cm from beg, ending with a purl row.

SHAPE TOP
Keeping Main Patt correct, cast off 5 (5-6-6-7) sts at beg of next 8 rows, then 5 (6-6-6-6) sts at beg of foll 2 rows.
Cast off rem 15 (17-17-19-19) sts loosely.

## Right front band
Using 3.25mm needles, cast on 8 sts.
**1ST ROW:** K3, P1, K1, P1, K2 (buttonhole).
**2ND ROW:** K1, (P1, K1) twice, P3.
Rep 1st and 2nd rows once.
** **5TH ROW:** K3, yfwd, K2tog, P1, K2 (buttonhole).
Rep 2nd row once, then 1st and 2nd rows 7 (6-7-7-8) times. **
Rep from ** to ** 4 (5-5-5-5) times, then 5th row once. 6 (7-7-7-7) buttonholes in all.
Rep 2nd row once, then 1st and 2nd rows once.
Cast off.

## Left front band
Using 3.25mm needles, cast on 8 sts.
**1ST ROW:** K2, P1, K1, P1, K3.
**2ND ROW:** P3, (K1, P1) twice, K1.
Rep 1st and 2nd rows 43 (45-51-51-57) times.
Cast off loosely.

## Collar
Using 4.00mm needles, cast on 155 (165-165-185-185) sts to work ruffle.
Work 14 rows of ruffle as given for Size 2

of Back, noting that there will be 125 (133-133-149-149) sts after 4th row, 95 (101-101-113-113) sts after 8th row and 65 (69-69-77-77) sts after 12th row.
Purl 1 row. Cast off loosely.

## To make up

Join shoulder seams. Tie markers 14 (15-16-17-19) cm down from beg of shoulder shaping on side edges of Back and Fronts to mark armholes. Sew in sleeves evenly between markers, placing centres of sleeves to shoulder seams. Join side and sleeve seams. Sew front bands in position, placing ribbed edge to garment. Using a flat seam, sew cast-off edge of collar evenly in position, beg and ending at centre of front bands. Sew on buttons.

# TEDDY'S HAT

Using set of 4.00mm needles, cast on 120 (170) sts to work ruffle.
**1st Round:** * P3, K7, rep from * to end. Rep 1st round twice.
**4th Round:** * P3, K2, sl2, K1, p2sso, K2, rep from * to end. 96 (136) sts.
**5th Round** * P3, K5, rep from * to end. Rep 5th round twice.
**8th Round:** * P3, K1, sl2, K1, p2sso, K1, rep from * to end. 72 (102) sts.
**9th Round:** * P3, K3, rep from * to end. Rep 9th round twice.
**12th Round:** * P3, sl2, K1, p2sso, rep from * to end. 48 (68) sts.
**13th Round:** * P3, K1, rep from * to end. Rep 13th round.
**15th Round (wrong side):** P2 (6), * inc

**Note:** *Always slip sts knitways in patt.*

purlways in next 1 (2) st/s, P1, rep from * to last 2 (5) sts, P2 (5). 70 (106) sts.
**16th Round:** * K1, P1, rep from * to end. Rep 16th round 11 (13) times.
Divide for back and front pieces
**Next Row:** Inc purlways in first st, P33 (51), inc in next st, turn.
Change to 4.00mm needles and cont on these 37 (55) sts for Back piece.

Begin Main Pattern
**Work 4 rows stocking st.
**5th Row:** K2 (3), * P1, K7, rep from * to last 3 (4) sts, P1, K2 (3).
Work 5 rows stocking st, beg with a purl row.
**11th Row:** K6 (7), * P1, K7, rep from * to last 7 (8) sts, P1, K6 (7).
**12th Row:** Purl.
Last 12 rows form Main Patt.
Work a further 0 (8) rows Main Patt.
Cast off.
Using 4.00mm needles, join yarn to rem sts, inc purlways in first st, P33 (51), inc purlways in last st, turn.
Cont on those 37 (55) sts for Front piece.
Complete as given for Back piece from ** to end.

## To make up

Join side and top seams of hat. Fold ruffle to right side and catch in position (if desired). Make a tassel (see Stitch Glossary) 4cm in length (finished). Using 4.00mm crochet hook, work a length of chain 4cm long in each corner at top of hat. Attach tassels to lengths of chain, as illustrated.

# Fair Isle cardigan & beret

*Measurements*

Years

| 1 | 2 | 3 | 4 | 6 |

Cardigan
To fit chest (cm):

| 52.5 | 55 | 57.5 | 60 | 65 |

Actual measurement (cm):

| 60 | 64 | 67 | 70 | 77 |

Length (cm):

| 36 | 38 | 40 | 42 | 46 |

Sleeve length (cm):

| 21 | 23 | 25 | 28 | 33 |

Beret
To fit head (approx) (cm):

| 49 | 51 | 51 | 52 | 52 |

*Materials*

Cleckheaton Country 8 ply or Country Naturals 8 ply (50g balls)
Cardigan
Main Colour (MC):

| 4 | 5 | 5 | 6 | 6 |

1st Contrast (C1):

| 1 | 1 | 2 | 2 | 2 |

2nd Contrast (C2):

| 2 | 2 | 3 | 3 | 4 |

3rd Contrast (C3):

| 1 | 1 | 1 | 1 | 1 |

4th Contrast (C4):

| 1 | 1 | 1 | 2 | 2 |

or Cleckheaton Machinewash 8 ply or Cleckheaton 8 ply Pure Wool (50g balls)
Main Colour (MC):

| 4 | 5 | 5 | 6 | 6 |

1st Contrast (C1):

| 1 | 1 | 1 | 2 | 2 |

2nd Contrast (C2):

| 2 | 2 | 3 | 3 | 4 |

3rd Contrast (C3):

| 1 | 1 | 1 | 1 | 1 |

4th Contrast (C4):

| 1 | 1 | 1 | 2 | 2 |

Beret
1 ball each MC, C1, C2, C3 and C4.

One pair each 3.25mm, 4.00mm and 4.50mm knitting needles for Cardigan and 1 set each of 3.25mm, 4.00mm and 4.50mm knitting needles for Beret, or the required size to give correct tension; knitter's needle for sewing seams; 6 (6-6-6-7) buttons for Cardigan.

## CARDIGAN

*Back*
Using 3.25mm needles and MC, cast on 69 (73-75-79-87) sts.
**1st Row:** K2, * P1, K1, rep from * to last st, K1.
**2nd Row:** K1, * P1, K1, rep from * to end.
Rep 1st and 2nd rows 5 (5-5-7-8) times, then 1st row once.
**Next Row (wrong side):** Rib 8 (10-10-12-6), * inc in next st, rib 9 (9-7-7-9), rep from * to last 1 (3-1-3-1) st/s, rib 1 (3-1-3-1). 75 (79-83-87-95) sts [14 (14-14-18-20) rows rib in all].
Change to 4.00mm needles and Beg Patt:

**Tension**
*These garments have been designed at a tension of 24 sts and 28 rows to 10cm over Fair Isle Patt, using needles as specified on Graphs.*

Rows 1 to 12 incl from Graph A form patt, noting needle changes.

Work in patt until work measures 22 (23-24-25-27) cm from beg, ending with a purl row.

Tie markers at each end of last row to mark beg of armholes as there is no armhole shaping.

Work a further 38 (40-44-46-52) rows patt.

SHAPE SHOULDERS

Keeping patt correct, cast off 9 (10-10-11-12) sts at beg of next 4 rows, then 9 (9-10-10-11) sts at beg of foll 2 rows.

Cast off rem 21 (21-23-23-25) sts loosely in patt.

## Left front

Using 3.25mm needles and MC, cast on 35 (37-37-39-43) sts.

Work 13 (13-13-17-19) rows rib as given for Back.

**NEXT ROW (WRONG SIDE):** Rib 10 (12-4-6-8), * inc in next st, rib 11 (11-7-7-7), rep from * to last 1 (1-1-1-3) st/s, rib 1 (1-1-1-3). 37 (39-41-43-47) sts [14 (14-14-18-20) rows rib in all].

Change to 4.00mm needles.

Work in patt as indicated on Graph A for Left Front until work measures same as back to armhole markers, ending with same patt row. **

Tie markers at end of last row to mark beg of armhole.

SHAPE FRONT

Keeping patt correct, dec one st at end (front edge) of next row and foll 4th rows until 27 (29-30-32-35) sts rem.

Work 1 (3-3-5-7) row/s patt.

SHAPE SHOULDER

Cast off 9 (10-10-11-12) sts at beg of next row and foll alt row.

Work 1 row. Cast off rem 9 (9-10-10-11) sts.

## Right front

Work as given for Left Front to **, working patt from Graph A as indicated for Right Front.

Tie markers at beg of last row to mark beg of armhole.

SHAPE FRONT

Keeping patt correct, dec one st at beg (front edge) of next and foll 4th rows until 27 (29-30-32-35) sts rem.

Work 2 (4-4-6-8) rows patt.

SHAPE SHOULDER

Cast off 9 (10-10-11-12) sts at beg of next row and foll alt row.

Work 1 row. Cast off rem 9 (9-10-10-11) sts.

## Sleeves

Using 3.25mm needles and MC, cast on 33 (37-37-39-39) sts.

Work 13 (13-13-17-19) rows rib as for Back.

**NEXT ROW (WRONG SIDE):** Rib 6 (8-6-6-2), * inc in next st, rib 1, rep from * to last 3 (5-3-5-1) st/s, rib 3 (5-3-5-1). 45 (49-51-53-57) sts.

Change to 4.00mm needles.

Work in patt from Graph A and noting to

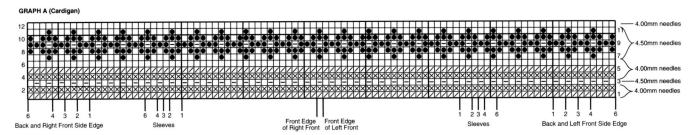

GRAPH A (Cardigan)

Back and Right Front Side Edge    Sleeves    Front Edge of Right Front    Front Edge of Left Front    Sleeves    Back and Left Front Side Edge

NOTE: When working from Graph A, read odd numbered rows (knit rows) from right to left and even numbered rows (purl rows) from left to right. Note needle changes on appropriate rows.

KEY
◉ = MC
⊠ = C1
☐ = C2
⊟ = C3
⊡ = C4

work extra sts into patt, inc one st at each end of 3rd and foll alt rows until there are 55 (55-61-61-65) sts, then in foll 4th rows until there are 69 (73-79-83-93) sts.
Cont in patt (without further inc) until work measures 21 (23-25-28-33) cm from beg, ending with a purl row.

SHAPE TOP
Keeping patt correct, cast off 5 (5-6-6-7) sts at beg of next 8 rows, then 6 (7-6-7-8) sts at beg of foll 2 rows.
Cast off rem 17 (19-19-21-21) sts loosely in patt.

## Left front band
(If making for girl, omit buttonholes).
Join shoulder seams. With right side facing, using 3.25mm needles and MC, knit up 50 (51-57-58-65) sts evenly from centre back neck to beg of front slope shaping, then 63 (68-68-73-80) sts evenly along rem of front edge. 113 (119-125-131-145) sts.
Work 3 rows rib as given for Back, beg with a 2nd row.
**4TH ROW:** Rib 52 (53-59-60-67), cast off 2 sts, [rib 9 (10-10-11-10), cast off 2 sts] 5 (5-5-5-6) times, rib 4.
**5TH ROW:** Rib 4, [cast on 2 sts, rib 9 (10-10-11-10)] 6 (6-6-6-7) times, rib to end. 6 (6-6-6-7) buttonholes.
Work 4 rows rib.
Cast off loosely in rib.

## Right front band
(If making for boy, omit buttonholes)
With right side facing, using 3.25mm needles and MC, knit up 63 (68-68-73-80) sts evenly along front edge to beg of front slope, then 50 (51-57-58-65) sts evenly along rem of front edge to centre of back neck. 113 (119-125-131-145) sts.
Work 3 rows rib as given for Back, beg with a 2nd row.
**4TH ROW:** Rib 4, [cast off 2 sts, rib 9 (10-10-11-10)] 6 (6-6-6-7) times, rib to end.
**5TH ROW:** Rib 52 (53-59-60-67), cast on 2 sts, [rib 9 (10-10-11-10), cast on 2 sts] 5 (5-5-5-6) times, rib 4. 6 (6-6-6-7) buttonholes.
Work 4 rows rib.
Cast off loosely in rib.

## To make up
Sew in sleeves evenly between markers, placing centres of sleeves to shoulder seams. Join side and sleeve seams. Join front band at centre back. Sew on buttons.

# BERET

Using set of 3.25mm needles and MC, cast on 86 (96-96-108-108) sts.
**1ST ROUND:** * K1, P1, rep from * to end.
Rep 1st round 9 times.
**11TH ROUND:** K2 (0-0-4-4), * inc in next st, K1, rep from * to end. 128 (144-144-160-160) sts.
Change to set of 4.00mm needles and Beg Patt:
Rounds 1 to 12 incl from Graph B form patt, noting needle changes.
Work 11 (11-11-17-17) rounds patt, beg with a 1st (1st-1st-7th-7th) round and thus ending with an 11th round.

SHAPE CROWN
Change to set of 4.00mm needles.
**1ST ROUND:** Using C2, K3, * K2tog, K6, rep from * to last 5 sts, K2tog, K3. 112 (126-126-140-140) sts.
**2ND ROUND:** Using C4, Knit.
**3RD ROUND:** K2, * K2tog, K5, rep from * to last 5sts, K2tog, K3. 96 (108-108-120-120) sts.
Change to set of 4.50mm needles.
**4TH ROUND:** K1C2, K1C3, rep from * to end.
Change to set of 4.00mm needles.
**5TH ROUND:** Using C1, K1, K2tog, K4, rep

**NOTE:** *Do not weave colours in Fair Isle Patt but carry colour not in use loosely across on wrong side of work. Always carry colours to end of rows and catch in at side edge. Always carry C2 above C3 and MC, and MC above C3.*

GRAPH B (Beret)

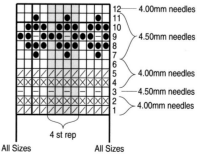

12 — 4.00mm needles
11
10
9 — 4.50mm needles
8
7
6
5 — 4.00mm needles
4
3 — 4.50mm needles
2 — 4.00mm needles
1

4 st rep

All Sizes      All Sizes

NOTE: When working from Graph B, read all rounds (knit rounds) from right to left. For each round, beg at right side and work to beg of rep, work rep across round until number of sts after the rep rem, then work these sts to end of round. Note needle changes at beg of appropriate round.

from * to last 5 sts, K2tog, K3. 80 (90-90-100-100) sts.

**6TH ROUND:** Using C4, knit.

**7TH ROUND:** Using C2, * K2tog, K3, rep from * to last 5 sts, K2tog, K3. 64 (72-72-80-80) sts.

Change to set of 4.50mm needles.

Work rows 7 to 11 incl from Graph B.

Rep last 12 rounds once, noting that there will be 32 (36-36-40-40) sts at end of 7th round.

Change to set of 4.00mm needles.

**25TH ROUND:** Using C2, K3, * K2tog, K2, rep from * to last st, K1. 25 (28-28-31-31) sts.

**26TH ROUND:** Using C4, knit.

**27TH ROUND:** Using C1, K2, * K2tog, K1, rep from * to last 2 sts, K2. 18 (20-20-22-22) sts.

Break off yarn, run end through rem sts, draw up and fasten off securely.

# Teddy's striped jacket

## Measurements

| | | |
|---|---|---|
| To fit chest (cm) | 36 | 55 |
| Actual measurement (cm): | 40 | 59 |
| Length (approx) (cm): | 13 | 18 |
| Sleeve length (cm): | 6 | 9 |

## Materials

Cleckheaton Country 8ply or Country
Naturals 8 ply (50g balls)

| | | |
|---|---|---|
| Main Colour (MC): | 1 | 2 |
| 1st Contrast (C1): | 1 | 1 |
| 2nd Contrast (C2): | 1 | 2 |

or Cleckheaton Machinewash 8 ply or
Cleckheaton 8 ply Pure Wool (50g balls)

| | | |
|---|---|---|
| Main Colour (MC): | 1 | 2 |
| 1st Contrast (C1): | 1 | 1 |
| 2nd Contrast (C2): | 1 | 1 |

One pair 4.00mm knitting needles or the
required size to give correct tension; 1
stitch holder; knitter's needle for sewing
seams; 5 (6) buttons.

## Back

Using 4.00mm needles and MC, cast on 44
(64) sts.
Knit 4 rows garter st (1st row is wrong
side), inc 3 sts evenly across last row. 47
(67) sts.
Work 6 rows stocking st in stripes of 2 rows
each C1, C2 and MC, beg with a purl row.
Last 6 rows form patt.
Cont in patt until work measures 11.5
(16.5) cm from beg, ending with a purl row.

SHAPE NECK
Keeping stripes correct, **NEXT ROW:** K17
(23), turn.
Cont on these 17 (23) sts.
Dec one st at neck edge in next 2 rows. 15
(21) sts.
Work 1 row. Cast off rem sts loosely.
Slip next 13 (21) sts onto stitch holder and
leave.
With right side facing, join appropriate
colour to rem sts and knit to end.
Cont on these 17 (23) sts.
Dec one st at neck edge in next 2 rows. 15
(21) sts.
Work 1 row.
Cast off rem sts loosely.

## Left front

Using 4.00mm needles and MC, cast on 22
(32) sts.
Knit 4 rows garter st (1st row is wrong
side), inc one st in centre of last row. 23
(33) sts.
Work throughout in patt as given for Back
(beg with a purl row) until there are 9 (15)
rows less than Back to cast-off edge, thus
ending with a knit row. **

SHAPE NECK
Keeping stripes correct, cast off 4 (6) sts at
beg of next row. 19 (27) sts.
Dec one st at neck edge in next and alt
rows until 15 (21) sts rem.
Work 1 (3) row/s.
Cast off loosely.

TENSION
*This garment has been
designed at a tension of
22 sts and 30 rows to
10cm over stocking st,
using 4.00mm needles.*
NOTE: *Do not break
off yarn when working
stripes, catch in on alt
rows.*

## Right front

Work as given for Left Front to **, noting to work 1 row less, thus ending with a purl row.

SHAPE NECK
Keeping stripes correct, cast off 4 (6) sts at beg of next row.  19 (27) sts.
Dec one st at neck edge in alt rows until 15 (21) sts rem.
Work 1 (3) row/s.
Cast off loosely.

## Neckband

Join shoulder seams.  With right side facing, using 4.00mm needles and MC, knit up  41 (61) sts evenly around neck, incl sts from stitch holder.
Knit 3 rows garter st.
Cast off loosely knitways.

## Right front band

With right side facing, using 4.00mm needles and MC, knit up 26 (36) sts evenly along edge of Right Front and across end of neckband.
Knit 1 row.
NEXT ROW:  K2, [yfwd, K2tog, K3 (4)] 4 (5) times, yfwd, K2tog, K2.  5 (6) buttonholes.
Knit 1 row.
Cast off loosely.

## Left front band

Work to correspond with Right Front Band, omitting buttonholes.

## To make up

Tie markers 7 (10) cm down from shoulder seams on side edges of Back and Fronts to mark armholes.  Sew in sleeves evenly between markers, placing centres of sleeves to shoulder seams.  Join side and sleeve seams.  Sew on buttons.

# ABC jumper

## Measurements

Years

| 1 | 2 | 3 | 4 | 6 |
|---|---|---|---|---|

Chest (cm):

| 52.5 | 55 | 57.5 | 60 | 65 |
|---|---|---|---|---|

Actual measurement (cm):

| 59 | 64 | 67 | 70 | 77 |
|---|---|---|---|---|

Length (approx) (cm):

| 36 | 38 | 40 | 42 | 46 |
|---|---|---|---|---|

Sleeve length (approx) (cm):

| 21 | 23 | 25 | 28 | 33 |
|---|---|---|---|---|

## Materials

Cleckheaton Cotton Soft 8ply ( 50g balls)

| 5 | 5 | 5 | 6 | 6 |
|---|---|---|---|---|

One pair 3.75mm knitting needles or the required size to give correct tension; 2 stitch holders; a 3.00mm crochet hook; knitter's needle for sewing seams and embroidery; DMC stranded cotton (see Graphs for shades and quantities); 3 buttons for shoulder opening.

## Back

Using 3.75mm needles, cast on 69 (75-79-83-91) sts.
Work 4 rows stocking st.
**Next Row (Picot edge):** K1, * yfwd, K2tog, rep from * to end. **
Work 109 (115-121-127-139) rows stocking st, beg with a purl row.

### Shape Shoulders
Cast off 7 (7-8-8-9) sts at beg of next 4 rows, then 7 (8-8-9-10) sts at beg of foll 2 rows.
Leave rem 27 (31-31-33-35) sts on a stitch holder.

## Front

Work as given for Back to **.
Work 97 (101-107-111-121) rows stocking st, beg with a purl row.

### Shape Neck
**Next Row:** K28 (30-32-34-37), turn.
Cont on these 28 (30-32-34-37) sts and dec one st at neck edge in every row until 24 (26-28-30-35) sts rem, then in alt rows until 21 (22-24-25-28) sts rem.
Work 1 row.

### Shape Shoulder
Cast off 7 (7-8-8-9) sts at beg of next row and foll alt row.
Work 1 row.
Cast off rem 7 (8-8-9-10) sts.
Slip next 13 (15-15-15-17) sts onto stitch holder and leave. With right side facing, join yarn to rem sts and knit to end.
Cont on these 28 (30-32-34-37) sts and dec one st at neck edge in every row until 24 (26-28-30-35) sts rem, then in alt rows until 21 (22-24-25-28) sts rem.
Work 2 rows.

### Shape Shoulder
Cast off 7 (7-8-8-9) sts at beg of next row and foll alt row.
Work 1 row. Cast off rem 7 (8-8-9-10) sts.

## Sleeves

Using 3.75mm needles, cast on 37 (39-41-43-45) sts.
Work 4 rows stocking st.
**Next Row (Picot edge):** K1, * yfwd, K2tog, rep from * to end.
Work 5 rows stocking st, beg with a purl row.

**Note:** Embroidery is worked on completion of knitting, using stranded cotton and Knitting Stitch Embroidery.

**Tension**
This garment has been designed at a tension of 23 sts and 31 rows to 10cm over stocking st, using 3.75mm needles.

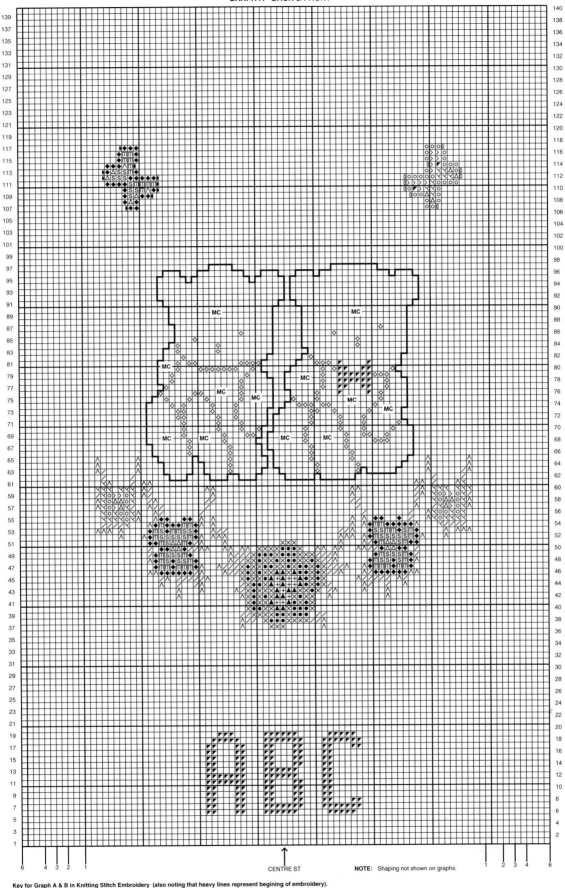

CENTRE ST

NOTE: Shaping not shown on graphs.

**Key for Graph A & B in Knitting Stitch Embroidery (also noting that heavy lines represent begining of embroidery).**

☐ = Cotton Soft, unless otherwise stated.

⊠ = Cotton Soft

☐ = MC - Beige (945 - 12 skeins)

◪ = Blue (3747 - 9 skeins)

◉ = Pale Pink (818 - 3 skeins)

⊠ = Light Pink (776 - 3 skeins)

⊞ = Medium Pink (899 - 3 skeins)

▲ = Dark Pink (335 - 2 skeins)

⊿ = Light Green (964 - 3 skeins)

⊼ = Dark Green (958 - 4 skeins)

Ⓢ = Light Lilac (211 - 3 skeins)

Ⅲ = Medium Lilac (544 - 3 skeins)

◈ = Dark Lilac (210 - 3 skeins)

△ = Lemon (445 - 2 skeins)

◹ = Light Peach (761 - 3 skeins)

▷ = Medium Peach (3708 - 3 skeins)

◻ = Dark Peach (3706 - 3 skeins)

▯ = Half stitch in nominated colour.

Cont in stocking st, inc one st at each end of next and alt row/s until there are 45 (47-51-47-49) sts, then in foll 4th rows until there are 67 (71-77-79-89) sts.
Work a further 11 (11-11-15-15) rows stocking st, beg with a purl row.

SHAPE TOP
Cast off 5 (6-6-6-7) st at beg of next 6 (8-6-6-6) rows, then 6 (5-7-7-8) sts at beg of foll 4 (2-4-4-4) rows.
Cast off rem 13 (13-13-15-15) sts.

## Neck edging

Join right shoulder seam. With right side facing and using 3.75mm needles, knit up 69 (79-79-85-93) sts evenly around neck, incl sts from stitch holders.
Work 3 rows stocking st, beg with a purl row.
**NEXT ROW (PICOT EDGE):** K1, * yfwd, K2tog, rep from * to end.
Work 3 rows stocking st, beg with a purl row.
Cast off loosely.

## To make up

Embroider Back and Front of jumper using DMC stranded cotton double from Graph A, noting that "ABC" begins 5 rows above picot row on all sizes and to place top of teddies 8 (10-12-14-16) rows below neck shaping. Note: Graph shows embroidery for Size 4.
Embroider sleeves from Graph B, noting that "C" begins 5 rows above picot row on all sizes and to leave 2 (2-4-6-8) rows between letters and flowers.
Using DMC stranded cotton work Stem St outlines on butterflies. Work a halo of Bullion St roses on teddy on right side of Jumper. Work Daisy St leaves to halo as illustrated. Embroider a Stem St branch either side of "ABC". Attach Daisy St leaves to branch. Work Bullion St roses at random to garment as illustrated.
Fold neckband in half onto wrong side at picot row and slip stitch loosely in position.
Join left shoulder seam for 3cm only from armhole edge to allow for shoulder opening. With right side facing and using 3.00mm hook, work 3 rows dc evenly around shoulder opening, working through both thicknesses of neck edging and working three 2ch buttonloops in 2nd row. Tie markers 14 (15-16-17-19) cm down from beg of shoulder shaping on side edges of Back and Front to mark armholes. Sew in sleeves evenly between markers, placing centres of sleeves to shoulder seams. Join side and sleeve seams. Fold hems at lower edge of Back, Front and Sleeves to wrong side at picot row and slip stitch loosely in position. Sew on buttons.

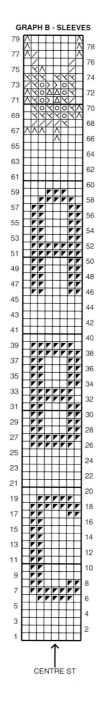

GRAPH B - SLEEVES

CENTRE ST

*Winter Fun*

# *Picot-edged jacket*

## Tension

*This garment has been designed at a tension of 22 sts and 28 rows to 10cm over Main Patt, using needles as specified on Graph B.*

**Note:** *Do not weave colours in Fair Isle patts but carry colours not in use loosely across on wrong side. It is important however, that no colour should be carried across more than 7 sts and where this is necessary (Graph A only) it should be woven under and over colour in use at centre st. Always carry colours to ends of rows and catch in at side edge. Always carry MC above contrasts, C1 above C2 and C3, and C2 above C3.*

## Measurements

| Years | | | | |
|---|---|---|---|---|
| 1 | 2 | 3 | 4 | 6 |

To fit chest (cm):

| | | | | |
|---|---|---|---|---|
| 52.5 | 55 | 57.5 | 60 | 65 |

Actual measurement (cm):

| | | | | |
|---|---|---|---|---|
| 60 | 64 | 67 | 70 | 77 |

Length (cm):

| | | | | |
|---|---|---|---|---|
| 36 | 38 | 40 | 42 | 46 |

Sleeve length (cm):

| | | | | |
|---|---|---|---|---|
| 21 | 23 | 25 | 28 | 33 |

## Materials

Cleckheaton Country or Country Naturals 8 ply (50g balls)

Main Colour (MC):

| | | | | |
|---|---|---|---|---|
| 5 | 6 | 6 | 7 | 7 |

1st Contrast (C1):

| | | | | |
|---|---|---|---|---|
| 1 | 1 | 1 | 1 | 1 |

2nd Contrast (C2):

| | | | | |
|---|---|---|---|---|
| 1 | 1 | 1 | 1 | 1 |

3rd Contrast (C3):

| | | | | |
|---|---|---|---|---|
| 1 | 1 | 1 | 1 | 1 |

or Cleckheaton Machinewash 8 ply or Cleckheaton 8 ply Pure Wool (50g balls)

Main Colour (MC):

| | | | | |
|---|---|---|---|---|
| 5 | 5 | 6 | 6 | 7 |

1st Contrast (C1):

| | | | | |
|---|---|---|---|---|
| 1 | 1 | 1 | 1 | 1 |

2nd Contrast (C2):

| | | | | |
|---|---|---|---|---|
| 1 | 1 | 1 | 1 | 1 |

3rd Contrast (C3):

| | | | | |
|---|---|---|---|---|
| 1 | 1 | 1 | 1 | 1 |

One pair each 4.00mm and 4.50mm knitting needles or the required size to give correct tension; a 3.50mm crochet hook; knitter's needle for sewing seams.

## Back

Using 4.00mm needles and MC, cast on 69 (73-75-79-87) sts.

Work 7 rows stocking st.

Using C1, purl 1 row.

Using MC, knit 1 row.

**Next Row:** P2 (4-5-7-11), * inc purlways in next st, P12, rep from * to last 2 (4-5-7-11) sts, inc purlways in next st, P1 (3-4-6-10). 75 (79-81-85-93) sts.

Change to 4.50mm needles.

Work rows 1 to 7 incl from Graph A.

Change to 4.00mm needles.

**Next Row:** Using MC, P2 (4-5-7-11), * P2tog, P12, rep from * to last 3 (5-6-8-12) sts, P2tog, P1 (3-4-6-10). 69 (73-75-79-87) sts.

** Knit 1 row.

Using C1, purl 1 row.

### Begin Main Pattern

Work rows 1 to 24 incl from Graph B, noting needle changes.

These 24 rows form Main Patt for rem.

Cont in Main Patt until work measures 21 (22-22-24-26) cm from beg, ending with a purl row. **

### Shape Armholes

Keeping Main Patt correct, cast off 7 (7-7-

7-8) sts at beg of next 2 rows.  55 (59-61-65-71) sts.
Work 36 (40-44-46-52) rows Main Patt.

SHAPE SHOULDERS
Cast off 6 (6-7-7-8) sts at beg of next 4 rows, then 6 (7-6-8-8) sts at beg of foll 2 rows.
Cast off rem 19 (21-21-21-23) sts loosely.

## Left front
Using 4.00mm needles and MC, cast on 33 (35-36-38-42) sts.
Work 7 rows stocking st.
Using C1, purl 1 row.
Using MC, knit 1 row.
**NEXT ROW:** P3 (4-5-6-8), * inc purlways in next st, P12, rep from * once, inc purlways in next st, P3 (4-4-5-7).  36 (38-39-41-45) sts.
Change to 4.50mm needles.
Work rows 1 to 7 incl from Graph A.
Change to 4.00mm needles.
**NEXT ROW:** Using MC, P3 (4-5-6-8), * P2tog, P12, rep from * once, P2tog, P3 (4-

4-5-7).  33 (35-36-38-42) sts.
Work as given for Back from ** to **, working  Graph B as indicated for Left Front. ***

SHAPE ARMHOLE
Keeping Main Patt correct, cast off 7 (7-7-7-8) sts at beg of next row.  26 (28-29-31-34) sts.
Work 26 (28-32-32-36) rows Main Patt.

SHAPE NECK
**NEXT ROW:**  Cast off 4 sts, patt to end.  22 (24-25-27-30) sts.
Dec one st at neck edge in next and alt rows until 18 (19-20-22-24) sts rem.
Work 3 (3-3-5-5) rows Main Patt.

SHAPE SHOULDER
Cast off 6 (6-7-7-8) sts at beg of next row and foll alt row.
Work 1 row.  Cast off rem 6 (7-6-8-8) sts.

## Right front
Work as given for Left Front to ***,

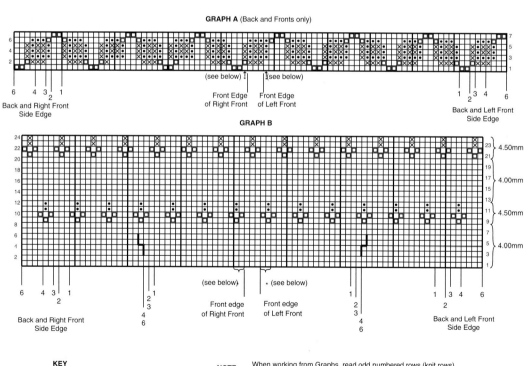

GRAPH A (Back and Fronts only)

(see below)          (see below)

6  4  3  1                          Front Edge      Front Edge                    1  2  3  4      6
         2                          of Right Front   of Left Front                   2

Back and Right Front                                                            Back and Left Front
Side Edge                                                                       Side Edge

GRAPH B

4.50mm
4.00mm
4.50mm
4.00mm

6  4  3  1          1              (see below)    * (see below)           1              1  3  4    6
         2          2                                                     2              2
                    3                                                     3
                    4                                                     4
                    6                                                     6

Back and Right Front     Front edge      Front edge                           Back and Left Front
Side Edge                of Right Front   of Left Front                        Side Edge

**KEY**

☐  = MC
◧  = C1
☒  = C2
⊡  = C3

**NOTE:**  When working from Graphs, read odd numbered rows (knit rows) from left to right and even numbered rows ( purl rows) from left to right.

*  When working Fronts, work these st/s in MC only ie omit flower patt at centre front edge.

**NOTE.**  Not all Sleeve shaping shown on Graph B.

working Graphs as indicated for Right Front.
Work 1 row.

SHAPE ARMHOLE
Keeping Main Patt correct, cast off 7 (7-7-7-8) sts at beg of next row. 26 (28-29-31-34) sts.
Work 24 (26-30-30-34) rows Main Patt.

SHAPE NECK
**NEXT ROW:** Cast off 4 sts, patt to end. 22 (24-25-27-30) sts.
Dec one st at neck edge in alt rows until 18 (19-20-22-24) sts rem.
Work 4 (4-4-6-6) rows Main Patt.

SHAPE SHOULDER
Cast off 6 (6-7-7-8) sts at beg of next row and foll alt row.
Work 1 row. Cast off rem 6 (7-6-8-8) sts.

## Sleeves
Using 4.00mm needles and MC, cast on 37 (39-39-41-41) sts.
Work throughout in Main Patt as given for Graph B, noting to beg with 3rd row of graph instead of first and at same time (noting to work extra sts into Main Patt) inc one st at each end of foll 3rd rows until there are 47 (61-73-59-63) sts, then in foll 4th row/s until there are 61 (69-75-77-85) sts.
Cont (without further inc) until work measures 19 (21-23-26-31) cm from beg, ending with a purl row.
Tie markers at each end of last row to mark end of sleeve seam.
Work a further 10 (10-10-10-12) rows Main Patt.

SHAPE TOP
Keeping Main Patt correct, cast off 5 (5-6-6-7) sts at beg of next 6 (8-8-8-6) rows, then 4 (6-5-6-6) sts at beg of foll 4 (2-2-2-4) rows.
Cast off rem 15 (17-17-17-19) sts.

## To make up
Join shoulder, side and sleeve seams to markers. Sew in sleeves evenly, placing centres of sleeves to shoulder seams and extra rows above markers to sts cast-off at armholes on Back and Fronts.

CROCHET EDGING
With right side facing, using 3.50mm hook and MC, and beg at centre back neck, work 2 rounds dc evenly around neck, fronts and lower edges, working 3dc in corners, taking care to keep work flat and having a number divisible by 3.
**NEXT ROUND:** 1ch,* 1dc in each of next 3dc, 3ch, sl st into first of these 3ch, rep from * to end. Slst in first 1ch at beg.
Fasten off.
Work same edging around lower edges of sleeves.

# Circular-yoked Argyle jumper

## Measurements

Years

| 1 | 2 | 3 | 4 | 6 |
|---|---|---|---|---|

To fit chest (cm):

| 52.5 | 55 | 57.5 | 60 | 65 |
|---|---|---|---|---|

Actual measurement (cm):

| 60 | 64 | 67 | 70 | 77 |
|---|---|---|---|---|

Length (cm):

| 36 | 38 | 40 | 42 | 46 |
|---|---|---|---|---|

Sleeve length (cm):

| 19 | 21 | 23 | 26 | 31 |
|---|---|---|---|---|

## Materials

Cleckheaton Country 8 ply or Country Naturals 8 ply (50g balls)

Main Colour (MC):

| 5 | 6 | 6 | 7 | 7 |
|---|---|---|---|---|

1st Contrast (C1):

| 1 | 1 | 1 | 1 | 1 |
|---|---|---|---|---|

2nd Contrast (C2):

| 1 | 1 | 1 | 1 | 1 |
|---|---|---|---|---|

3rd Contrast (C3):

Small quantity

or Cleckheaton Machinewash 8 ply or Cleckheaton 8 ply Pure Wool (50g balls)

Main Colour (MC):

| 5 | 5 | 6 | 6 | 7 |
|---|---|---|---|---|

1st Contrast (C1):

| 1 | 1 | 1 | 1 | 1 |
|---|---|---|---|---|

2nd Contrast (C2):

| 1 | 1 | 1 | 1 | 1 |
|---|---|---|---|---|

3rd Contrast (C3):

Small quantity

One pair each 3.25mm and 4.00mm knitting needles, one 4.00mm circular needle (60cm long) or the required size to give correct tension; 4 stitch holders; knitter's needle for sewing seams and embroidery; Sizes 1, 2 and 3 only - a 3.50mm crochet hook and 3 buttons for raglan opening.

## Back

Using 3.25mm needles and MC, cast on 69 (73-75-79-87) sts.

**1st Row:** K2, * P1, K1, rep from * to last st, K1.

**2nd Row:** K1, * P1, K1, rep from * to end. Rep 1st and 2nd rows 5 (6-6-8-8) times. 12 (14-14-18-18) rows rib in all.

Change to 4.00mm needles.

Work in stocking st until work measures 21 (22-23-24-26) cm from beg, ending with a purl row.

### Shape Raglan Armholes

Cast off 2 (2-2-2-3) sts at beg of next 2 rows. 65 (69-71-75-81) sts. **

Dec one st at each end of next and alt row/s until 61 (63-65-67-71) sts rem.

Work 1 row.

### Shape Back

**1st Row:** K2tog, K18, turn.

**2nd and Alt Rows:** Purl to end.

**3rd Row:** K2tog, K12, turn.

**5th Row:** K2tog, K6, turn.

**7th Row:** K2tog, knit across all sts to last 2 sts, K2tog.

## Tension

*This garment has been designed at a tension of 22 sts and 30 rows to 10cm over stocking st, using 4.00mm needles.*

**Note:** *When turning, take yarn under needle and onto other side of work, slip next st onto right-hand needle, take yarn under needle and back to original position, slip st back onto left-hand needle, then turn and proceed as instructed. This avoids holes in work.*

Hat, shirts, pants and shoes from Osh Kosh B'Gosh. Toys from Hide & Seek. Teddies from The Teddy Bear Shop and Teddy & Friends.

Proceed as folls.

**1st Row:** P19, turn.

**2nd and Alt Rows:** Knit to last 2 sts, K2tog.

**3rd Row:** P13, turn.

**5th Row:** P7, turn.

**7th Row:** Purl across all sts to end, dec 4 (2-4-0-4) sts evenly across.

Leave rem 49 (53-53-59-59) sts on stitch holder.

## Front

Work as given for Back to **.

Sizes 2 and 3 only: dec one st at each end

of next row. Work 1 row.

Sizes 4 and 6 only: dec one st at each end of next and alt row/s until (71-75) sts rem. Work 1 row.

All sizes: 65 (67-69-71-75) sts.

SHAPE FRONT

**1st Row:** K2tog, K20, turn.

**2nd and Alt Rows:** Purl to end.

**3rd Row:** K2tog, K16, turn.

**5th Row:** K2tog, K12, turn.

**7th Row:** K2tog, K8, turn.

**9th Row:** K2tog, K4, turn.

**11th Row:** K2tog, knit across all sts to last

## Sleeves

Using 3.25mm needles and MC, cast on 33 (35-37-39-39) sts.

Work 12 (14-14-18-18) rows rib as given for Back, inc 4 (6-8-8-10) sts evenly across last row. 37 (41-45-47-49) sts.

Change to 4.00mm needles.

Work 4 rows stocking st.

**5TH ROW:** K2, M1, knit to last 2 sts, M1, K2.

Cont in stocking st, inc one st (as before) at each end of foll 4th (4th-6th-6th-8th) row/s until there are 43 (45-53-51-61) sts, then in foll 6th (6th-8th-8th-10th) rows until there are 51 (55-59-61-65) sts.

Cont (without further inc) until work measures 19 (21-23-26-31) cm from beg, ending with a purl row.

### SHAPE RAGLAN

Cast off 2 (2-2-2-3) sts at beg of next 2 rows. 47 (51-55-57-59) sts.

Dec one st at each end of next and alt rows until 35 (37-41-41-41) sts rem.

Work 1 row, dec 4 (0-4-0-0) sts evenly across.

Leave rem 31 (37-37-41-41) sts on stitch holder.

## Yoke

Join raglan seams, leaving left back raglan open. Slip sts from stitch holders onto 4.00mm circular needle, so that right side will be facing for first row. 160 (180-180-200-200) sts.

**NOTE:** Work in rows not rounds.

Using MC, work 6 (2-4-2-6) rows stocking st.

**NEXT ROW:** K11 (13-13-14-14), * K2tog, K6 (7-7-8-8), rep from * to last 5 (5-5-6-6) sts, K5 (5-5-6-6). 142 (162-162-182-182) sts.

Work 1 (1-3-1-1) row/s stocking st, beg with a purl row.

### BEGIN DIAMOND PATTERN

**1ST ROW:** K7 (8-8-9-9) MC, * K1C1, K13 (15-15-17-17) MC, K1C2, K13 (15-15-17-17) MC, rep from * to end, ending last rep K8 (9-9-10-10) MC instead of K13 (15-15-17-17) MC.

**NOTE:** *When changing colours in centre of row, twist the colour to be used underneath and to the right of colour just used, making sure both yarns are worked firmly at joins. Always change colours on wrong side of work so colour change does not show on right side. Use a separate ball of yarn for each section of colour. Wind yarn into smaller balls or onto bobbins if necessary.*

2 sts, K2tog.

Proceed as folls.

**1ST ROW:** P21, turn.

**2ND AND ALT ROWS:** Knit to last 2 sts, K2tog.

**3RD ROW:** P17, turn.

**5TH ROW:** P13, turn.

**7TH ROW:** P9, turn.

**9TH ROW:** P5, turn.

**11TH ROW:** Purl across all sts to end, dec 4 (2-4-0-4) sts evenly across.

Leave rem 49 (53-53-59-59) sts on stitch holder.

**2ND ROW:** Purl in colours as placed in previous row.

**3RD ROW:** K6 (7-7-8-8) MC, * K3C1, K11 (13-13-15-15) MC, K3C2, K11 (13-13-15-15) MC, rep from * to end, ending last rep K7 (8-8-9-9) MC, instead of K11 (13-13-15-15) MC.

Keeping C1 and C2 diamonds correct as for Graph A (B-B-C-C) as placed in last 3 rows, noting to beg with a 4th row and that there are 2 extra sts between diamonds at this point to allow for yoke shaping, work 3 rows.

**7TH ROW:** K2 (3-3-4-4) MC, * K2tog MC,

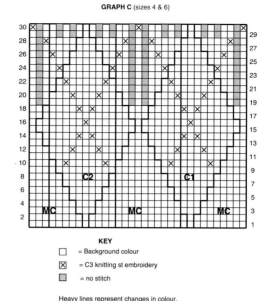

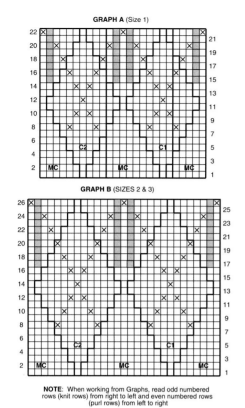

**GRAPH A** (Size 1)

**GRAPH B** (SIZES 2 & 3)

**GRAPH C** (sizes 4 & 6)

**NOTE**: When working from Graphs, read odd numbered rows (knit rows) from right to left and even numbered rows (purl rows) from left to right

** Graphs DO NOT show extra sts at start of graph which are dec on the 7th row

**KEY**

☐  =  background colour

☒  =  C3 knitting st embroidery

▨  =  no stitch

Heavey lines represent
changes in colour

**KEY**

☐  =  Background colour

☒  =  C3 knitting st embroidery

▨  =  no stitch

Heavy lines represent changes in colour.

K7C1, K2tog MC, K3 (5-5-7-7) MC, K2tog MC, K7C2, K2tog MC, K3 (5-5-7-7) MC, rep from * to end, ending last rep K3 (4-4-5-5) MC, instead of K3 (5-5-7-7) MC. 122 (142-142-162-162) sts.

Keeping C1 and C2 diamonds correct as for Graph A (B-B-C-C), noting to beg with an 8th row, work 9 (11-11-13-13) rows.

**Next Row:** K1MC, * K2tog MC, K1MC, K5 (7-9-9) C1, (K1MC, K2tog MC) twice, K1MC, K5 (7-9-9) C2, K1MC, K2tog MC, K1MC, rep from * to last st, K1MC. 102 (122-122-142-142) sts.

Keeping C1 and C2 diamonds correct as for Graph A (B-B-C-C), noting to beg with an 18th (20th-20th-22nd-22nd) row and that there are 2 less sts between diamonds at this point due to yoke shaping, work 3 (5-5-7-7) rows.

**Next Row:** K2 (3-3-4-4) MC, * K2tog MC, K1MC, K1C1, K1MC, K2tog MC,

K3 (5-5-7-7) MC, K2tog MC, K1MC, K1C2, K1MC, K2tog MC, K3 (5-5-7-7) MC, rep from * to end, ending last rep K3 (4-4-5-5) MC, instead of K3 (5-5-7-7) MC. 82 (102-102-122-122) sts.

**Next Row:** P5 (6-6-7-7) MC, * P1C2, P7 (9-9-11-11) MC, P1C1, P7 (9-9-11-11) MC, rep from * to end, ending last rep P4 (5-5-6-6) MC, instead of P7 (9-9-11-11) MC (thus completing Graph).

**Next Row:** Using MC for rem, K2 (3-3-2-2), * K2tog, K3 (2-2-1-1), K2tog, K3 (1-1-1-1), rep from * to last 0 (1-1-0-0) st/s, K0 (1-1-0-0). 66 (74-74-82-82) sts.

**Next Row:** Purl, dec one st in centre. 65 (73-73-81-81) sts.

Change to 3.25mm needles.

Work 8 rows rib as given for Back.

Cast off loosely in rib.

## *To make up*

Join left back raglan seam. Sizes 1, 2 and 3 only: noting to join for 4cm only from beg of armholes, then with right side facing and using 3.50mm hook and MC, work 2 rows dc evenly around raglan opening, working three 3ch buttonloops in 2nd row evenly along Back edge of raglan. Sew on buttons. All sizes: using Graph A (B-B-C-C) as a guide, work C3 embroidery (Knitting Stitch) to yoke. Join side and sleeve seams.

# Teddy's Argyle collar & teddy's socks

**TENSION**

*These items have been designed at a tension of 22 sts and 30 rows to 10cm over stocking st, using 4.00mm needles.*

**ABBREVIATIONS**

*Crab St = work as for dc but work from left to right instead of right to left so that sts are worked backwards.*

*Measurements*

Collar

| | | |
|---|---|---|
| To fit neck (approx) (cm): | 23 | 30 |
| Width (approx) (cm): | 9 | 11 |

Socks

| | | |
|---|---|---|
| Length | 10 | 14 |
| (with top turned back) (cm) | | |

*Materials*

Cleckheaton Country 8 ply or Country Naturals 8 ply or Cleckheaton Machinewash 8 ply or Cleckheaton 8 ply Pure Wool (50g balls)
1 ball each Main Colour (MC), 1st Contrast (C1), 2nd Contrast (C2) and 3rd Contrast (C3).

One pair 4.00mm knitting needles or the required size to give correct tension; a 3.25mm crochet hook; 1 small button.

## COLLAR

1ST DIAMOND

Using 4.00mm needles and C1, cast on 2 sts.

**1ST ROW:** K2.
**2ND ROW:** P2.
**3RD ROW:** K1, M1, K1. 3 sts.
**4TH ROW:** P3.
**5TH ROW:** Inc in first st, K1, inc in last st.

5 sts.
**6TH ROW:** P5.
**7TH ROW:** Inc in first st, K3, inc in last st.
7 sts.
Cont inc at each end of alt rows until there are 11 (13) sts.
**NEXT ROW:** P11 (13).
Break off yarn, leaving a long end to complete diamond shape. Leave sts on needle.

2ND DIAMOND

Using C2, cast on 2 sts to needle holding 1st Diamond.
Work as for 1st Diamond, leaving sts on needle holding 1st Diamond.

3RD DIAMOND

Using C1, cast on 2 sts to needle holding 1st and 2nd Diamonds.
Work as for 1st Diamond, leaving sts on needle holding 1st and 2nd Diamonds.
Cont making diamonds in this manner (alternating colours) until there are 9 diamonds on needle, thus beg and ending with a C1 diamond.

**NOTE:** When changing colours in centre of row, twist the colour to be used underneath and to the right of colour just used, making sure both yarns are worked firmly at joins. Always change colours on wrong side of work so colour change does not show on right side. Use a separate length of yarn for each section of colour.

**Next Row:** K1MC, K9 (11) C1, * K2MC, K9 (11) C2, K2MC, K9 (11) C1, rep from * to last st, K1MC. 99 (117) sts.
**Next Row:** P1MC, P9 (11) C1, * P2MC, P9 (11) C2, P2MC, P9 (11) C1, rep from * to last st, P1MC.
**Next Row:** K2MC, K7 (9) C1, * K1MC, K2tog MC, K1MC, K7 (9) C2, K1MC, K2tog MC, K1MC, K7 (9) C1, rep from * to last 2 sts, K2MC. 91 (109) sts.
**Next Row:** P2MC, P7 (9) C1, * P3MC, P7 (9) C2, P3MC, P7 (9) C1, rep from * to last 2 sts, P2MC.
**Next Row:** K3MC, K5 (7) C1, * K5MC, K5 (7) C2, K5MC, K5 (7) C1, rep from * to last 3 sts, K3MC.
Keeping diamonds correct as for Graph A (B) as placed, work a further 5 (7) rows, thus completing diamonds.
**Next Row:** Using MC for rem, K6 (7), * sl1, K2tog, psso, K3 (5), sl1, K2tog, psso, K1, rep from * to last 5 (6) sts, K5 (6). 59 (77) sts.
**Next Row:** P3 (7), * P2tog, P5, rep from * to end. 51 (67) sts.
Cast off loosely knitways.

## To make up

Embroider C3 detail from Graph A (B) to diamonds. Using crochet hook and MC, work 1 row dc, then 1 row Crab St evenly along outer edge of diamonds, taking care to keep work flat. Work a 3ch buttonloop at neck edge. Sew on button.

## SOCKS (Make 2)

Using 4.00mm needles and C1, cast on 30 (37) sts.
Work in garter st until work measures 12 (16) cm from beg.
Break off yarn (leaving an end of 10cm) and leave sts on needle.

## To make up
Thread end of yarn through all sts on needle and pull tightly to gather. Fasten off. Sew side seams of socks to form a tube, reversing seam for 2cm.

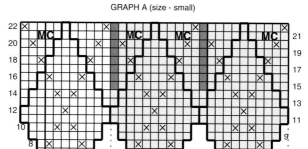

GRAPH A (size - small)

Work these sts 4 times in all

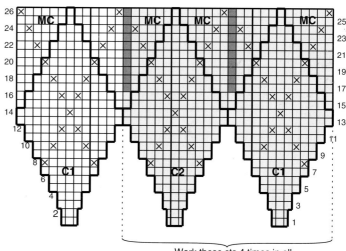

GRAPH B (size - large)

Work these sts 4 times in all

**NOTE:** When working from Graphs, read odd numbered rows (knit rows) from right to left and even numbered rows (purl rows) from left to right.

**KEY**

☐ = background colour

☒ = C3 "Knitting st" embroidery

▨ = no stitch

Heavy lines represent changes in colour

# *Teddy's waistcoat*

### TENSION

*These garments have been designed at a tension of 21 sts and 44 rows to 10cm over garter st, using 4.00mm needles.*

## *Measurements*

| | | |
|---|---|---|
| To fit chest (cm): | 36 | 55 |
| Actual measurement (cm): | 40 | 59 |
| Length (including points) (cm): | 10 | 17 |

## *Materials*

Waistcoat in One Colour
Cleckheaton Country 8 ply or Country Natural 8 ply or Cleckheaton Machinewash 8 ply or Cleckheaton 8 ply Pure Wool (50g balls)

| | |
|---|---|
| 1 | 2 |

Waistcoat in Stripes
Scraps of any of the above in 4 contrasting colours.

One pair 4.00mm knitting needles or the required size to give correct tension; knitter's needle for sewing seams; 3 buttons.

## WAISTCOAT IN ONE COLOUR

### *Back*

Using 4.00mm needles, cast on 45 (65) sts. Working in garter st (every row knit) throughout, work 7 (17) rows (1st row is wrong side).

#### SHAPE ARMHOLES

Cast off 4 (7) sts at beg of next 2 rows. 37 (51) sts.
Dec one st at each end of next and foll alt rows until 29 (39) sts rem.
Knit 17 (29) rows.

#### SHAPE BACK NECK

**NEXT ROW:** K9 (11), cast off next 11 (17) sts, knit to end.

Cont on last 9 (11) sts and dec one st at neck edge in every row 3 times.
Cast off rem 6 (8) sts.
With wrong side facing, join to rem 9 (11) sts and dec one st at neck edge in every row 3 times.
Cast off rem 6 (8) sts.

### *Left front*

Using 4.00mm needles, cast on 2 sts. Working in garter st throughout , knit 1 row (this row is wrong side). Inc one st at each end of every row until there are 16 (24) sts.
Knit 1 row. **
Cast on 5 (6) sts at beg of next row, then 3 (4) st at beg of foll row. 24 (34) sts.
Knit 6 (16) rows.

#### SHAPE ARMHOLE

Cast off 4 (7) sts at beg of next row. 20 (27) sts.
Dec one st at armhole edge in alt rows until 16 (21) sts rem.
Knit 1 row.

#### SHAPE FRONT SLOPE

Dec one st at end (front edge) of next and foll alt rows until 6 (8) sts rem.
Knit 1 (7) row/s.
Cast off rem sts.

### *Right front*

Work as given for Left Front to **.
Cast on 3 (4) sts at beg of next row, then 5 (6) sts at beg of foll row. 24 (34) sts.
Knit 2 rows.
**NEXT ROW:** K2, yfwd, K2 tog, knit to end (buttonhole).
Knit 4 (14) rows. Large size only: work a buttonhole (as before) in 12th row.

SHAPE ARMHOLE
Cast off 4 (7) sts at beg of next row.  20 (27) sts.
Dec one st at armhole edge in next and foll alt rows until 16 (21) sts rem, at same time working a buttonhole in foll 6th (12th) row/s from previous buttonhole 2 (1) time/s.
Knit 1 row.

SHAPE FRONT SLOPE
Dec one st at beg (front edge) of next and foll alt rows until 6 (8) sts rem.
Knit 1 (7) row/s.
Cast off rem sts.

*To make up*
Join shoulder and side seams.  Sew on buttons.

# FOR WAISTCOAT IN STRIPES

Before beginning to Knit, cut 60cm lengths of each colour and knot firmly tog in repeating sequence, leaving 1cm ends. Cont in this manner, winding lengths into a ball for ease, until ball weighs approx 40 (60) g.  Work as for Waistcoat in One Colour.  Do not darn in 1cm ends.

# Striped polo top

## TENSION

*This garment has been designed at a tension of 22 sts and 30 rows to 10cm over stocking st, using 4.00mm needles.*

## Measurements

| Years | | | | |
|---|---|---|---|---|
| 1 | 2 | 3 | 4 | 6 |

To fit chest (cm):

| 52.5 | 55 | 57.5 | 60 | 65 |
|---|---|---|---|---|

Actual measurement (cm):

| 60 | 64 | 67 | 70 | 77 |
|---|---|---|---|---|

Length (cm):

| 36 | 38 | 40 | 42 | 46 |
|---|---|---|---|---|

Sleeve length (cm):

| 21 | 23 | 25 | 28 | 33 |
|---|---|---|---|---|

## Materials

Cleckheaton Country 8 ply or Country Naturals 8 ply (50g balls)

1st Contrast (C1) navy:

| 2 | 2 | 3 | 3 | 3 |
|---|---|---|---|---|

2nd Contrast (C2) yellow:

| 1 | 1 | 1 | 2 | 2 |
|---|---|---|---|---|

3rd Contrast (C3) blue:

| 1 | 1 | 1 | 2 | 2 |
|---|---|---|---|---|

4th Contrast (C4) red:

| 1 | 1 | 2 | 2 | 2 |
|---|---|---|---|---|

5th Contrast (C5) green:

| 2 | 2 | 2 | 3 | 3 |
|---|---|---|---|---|

or Cleckheaton Machinewash 8ply or Cleckheaton 8 ply Pure Wool (50g balls)

1st Contrast (C1) navy:

| 1 | 2 | 2 | 2 | 2 |
|---|---|---|---|---|

2nd Contrast (C2) yellow:

| 1 | 1 | 1 | 2 | 2 |
|---|---|---|---|---|

3rd Contrast (C3) blue:

| 1 | 1 | 1 | 2 | 2 |
|---|---|---|---|---|

4th Contrast (C4) red:

| 1 | 1 | 1 | 1 | 1 |
|---|---|---|---|---|

5th Contrast (C5) green:

| 1 | 1 | 2 | 2 | 2 |
|---|---|---|---|---|

One pair each 3.25mm and 4.00mm knitting needles or the required size to give correct tension; knitter's needle for sewing seams; 2 buttons.

## Back

Using 3.25mm needles and C5, cast on 65 (69-73-75-83) sts.

**1ST ROW:** K2, * P1, K1, rep from * to last st, K1.

**2ND ROW:** K1, * P1, K1, rep from * to end.

Rep 1st and 2nd rows 6 (6-6-8-9) times, inc 4 sts evenly across last row. 69 (73-77-79-87) sts [14 (14-14-18-20) rows ribs in all]. Change to 4.00mm needles.

Work 64 (68-72-76-80) rows stocking st in stripes of 10 (10-12-12-12) rows C1, 4 (6-6-6-6) rows C2, 8 (8-8-10-10) rows C3, 4 rows C4, 6 (6-6-6-8) rows C5, 4 rows C1, 10 (10-12-12-12) rows C2, 4 (6-6-6-6) rows C3, 8 (8-8-10-10) rows C4 and 6 (6-6-6-8) rows C5.

Last 64 (68-72-76-80) rows form stripe patt.

Cont in stripe patt until work measures 35 (37-39-41-45) cm from beg, ending with a purl row.

### SHAPE SHOULDERS

**NOTE:** Do not commence another stripe during shoulder shaping but cont using colour of previous row.

Cast off 7 (8-8-9-10) sts at beg of next 4 rows, then 8 (7-9-8-9) sts at beg of foll 2 rows.

Cast off rem 25 (27-27-27-29) sts loosely.

## Front

Work as given for Back until there are 26 (28-28-32-34) rows less than Back to beg of shoulder shaping, thus ending with a purl row.

DIVIDE FOR FRONT OPENING

**NEXT ROW:** Keeping stripe patt correct throughout as for Back, K32 (34-36-37-41), cast off next 5 sts, knit to end.
Cont on last 32 (34-36-37-41) sts.
Work 13 (13-13-17-17) rows stripe patt.

SHAPE NECK

Cast off 4 sts at beg of next row. 28 (30-32-33-37) sts.
Work 1 row.
Dec one st at neck edge in every row until 25 (27-29-30-34) sts rem, then in alt rows until 22 (23-25-26-29) sts rem.
Work 2 rows stripe patt.

SHAPE SHOULDER

Cast off 7 (8-8-9-10) sts at beg of next row and foll alt row.
Work 1 row. Cast off rem 8 (7-9-8-9) sts.
With wrong side facing, join yarn to rem sts and purl to end.
Cont on these 32 (34-36-37-41) sts.
Work 13 (13-13-17-17) rows stripe patt.

SHAPE NECK

Cast off 4 sts at beg of next row. 28 (30-32-33-37) sts.
Dec one st at neck edge in every row until 25 (27-29-30-34) sts rem, then in alt rows until 22 (23-25-26-29) sts rem.
Work 1 row.

SHAPE SHOULDER

Cast off 7 (8-8-9-10) sts at beg of next row and foll alt row.
Work 1 row. Cast off rem 8 (7-9-8-9) sts.

## Sleeves

Using 3.25mm needles and C5, cast on 33 (35-37-37-39) sts.
Work 14 (14-14-18-20) rows rib as given for Back, inc 8 (8-10-10-12) sts evenly across last row. 41 (43-47-47-51) sts.
Change to 4.00mm needles.
Work throughout in stripe patt as given for Back, inc one st at each end of 5th and foll alt (alt-alt-alt-4th) row/s until there are 51 (51-53-51-83) sts, then in foll 4th (4th-4th-4th-6th) row/s until there are 65 (69-75-77-85) sts.
Cont in stripe patt (without further inc) until work measures 21 (23-25-28-33) cm from beg, ending with a purl row.

SHAPE TOP

**NOTE:** Do not commence another stripe in last 4 rows of shaping but cont using colour of previous row.

Cast off 6 (6-7-7-8) sts at beg of next 8 rows.
Cast off rem 17 (21-19-21-21) sts.

## Left front band

(If making for girl omit buttonholes)
Using 3.25mm needles and C1, knit up 15 (15-15-19-19) sts evenly along left side of front opening.
Work 3 rows rib as given for Back, beg with a 2nd row. **
**4TH ROW:** Rib 3, * cast off 2 sts, rib 4 (4-4-6-6), rep from * once.
**5TH ROW:** * Rib 4 (4-4-6-6), cast on 2 sts, rep from * once, rib 3. 2 buttonholes.
Work 5 rows rib.
Cast off loosely in rib.

## Right front band

(If making for boy, omit buttonholes)
Work as for Left Front Band to **, knitting sts up along right side of front opening.
**4TH ROW:** * Rib 4 (4-4-6-6), cast off 2 sts, rep from * once, rib 3.
**5TH ROW:** Rib 3, * cast on 2 sts, rib 4 (4-4-6-6), rep from * once. 2 buttonholes.
Work 5 rows rib.
Cast off loosely in rib.

## Collar

Using 3.25mm needles and C1, cast on 87 (99-99-99-105) sts.
Work 5 (5-5-6-6) cm rib as given for Back, ending with a 2nd row.
**NEXT ROW:** Rib 3, * ybk, sl1, K2tog, psso, rib 3, rep from * to end. 59 (67-67-67-71) sts.
Keeping rib correct, cast off 4 (5-5-5-5) sts at beg of next 8 rows. 27 (27-27-27-31) sts.
Cast off rem sts loosely in rib.

## To make up

Tie markers 14 (15-16-17-19) cm down from beg of shoulder shaping on side edges of Back and Front to mark armholes. Join shoulder seams. Sew in sleeves evenly between markers, placing centres of sleeves to shoulder seams. Join side and sleeve seams, carefully matching stripes. Slip stitch lower edge of front bands in position at centre front, so that buttonhole band is on top. Using a flat seam, sew cast off edge of collar in position, beg and ending at centre of front bands. Sew on buttons.

*Bridle Trail*

# Guernsey-style jumper

**TENSION**

*This garment has been designed at a tension of 22 sts and 30 rows to 10cm over stocking st, using 4.00mm needles.*

## Measurements

| Years | | | | |
|---|---|---|---|---|
| 1 | 2 | 3 | 4 | 6 |

To fit chest (cm):

| 52.5 | 55 | 57.5 | 60 | 65 |
|---|---|---|---|---|

Actual measurement (cm):

| 60 | 64 | 67 | 70 | 77 |
|---|---|---|---|---|

Length(approx) (cm):

| 36 | 38 | 40 | 42 | 46 |
|---|---|---|---|---|

Sleeve length (cm):

| 21 | 23 | 25 | 28 | 33 |
|---|---|---|---|---|

## Materials

Cleckheaton Country 8 ply or
Country Naturals 8 ply or Cleckheaton
Machinewash 8 ply or Cleckheaton 8 ply
Pure Wool (50g balls)

| 6 | 7 | 7 | 8 | 9 |
|---|---|---|---|---|

One pair 4.00mm and one set 3.25mm knitting needles or the required size to give correct tension; 2 stitch holders; knitter's needle for sewing seams.

## Back

Using 4.00mm needles, cast on 69 (73-75-79-87) sts using method for Guernsey edge (see Stitch Glossary).
Work rows 1 to 25 incl from Graph, noting that 1st row is a knit row on wrong side.
Work in stocking st until work measures 20 (22-23-24-26) cm from beg, ending with a knit row.
Work rows 1 to 18 incl from Graph.

Rows 7 to 18 incl form texture patt (last 12 rows).
Work 13 (13-19-19-25) rows texture patt.

### BEGIN YOKE PATTERN

Work rows 20 to 25 incl from Graph.
Last 6 rows form Yoke Patt for rem. **
Work a further 20 (22-22-24-26) rows Yoke Patt.

### SHAPE SHOULDERS

Keeping Yoke Patt correct, cast off 6 (7-7-7-8) sts at beg of next 4 rows, then 7 (6-7-7-8) sts at beg of foll 2 rows.
Leave rem 31 (33-33-37-39) sts on a stitch holder.

## Front

Work as given for Back to **.
Work a further 2 rows Yoke Patt.

### SHAPE NECK

**NEXT ROW:** Patt 27 (29-30-31-35), turn.
Keeping Yoke Patt correct, cont on these 27 (29-30-31-35) sts and dec one st at neck edge in alt rows until 19 (20-21-21-24) sts rem.
Work 1 row.

### SHAPE SHOULDER

Cast off 6 (7-7-7-8) sts at beg of next row and foll alt row.
Work 1 row. Cast off rem 7 (6-7-7-8) sts.
Slip next 15 (15-15-17-17) sts onto stitch holder and leave. With right side facing, join yarn to rem sts and patt to end.

Keeping Yoke Patt correct, cont on these 27 (29-30-31-35) sts and dec one st at neck edge in alt rows until 19 (20-21-21-24) sts rem.

Work 2 rows.

SHAPE SHOULDER

Cast off 6 (7-7-7-8) sts at beg of next row and foll alt row.

Work 1 row. Cast off rem 7 (6-7-7-8) sts.

## Sleeves

Using 4.00mm needles, cast on 37 (37-39-39-43) sts using method for Guernsey Edge (see Stitch Glossary).

Work rows 1 to 25 incl from Graph as placed for Size 2 (2-3-3-4) of Back and Front, at same time (noting to work extra sts into patt) inc one st at each end of 10th and foll 3rd (3rd-3rd-3rd-4th) rows until there are 49 (49-51-51-51) sts.

Working in stocking st, inc one st at each end of 3rd (3rd-3rd-3rd-1st) row and foll 4th (4th-3rd-3rd-4th) rows until there are 65 (67-65-57-79) sts, Sizes 3, 4 and 6 only: then inc in foll (4th-4th-6th) rows until there are (75-77-83) sts.

All sizes: cont (without further inc) until work measures 20 (22-24-27-32) cm from beg, ending with a purl row.

SHAPE TOP

NOTE: When turning take yarn under needle and onto other side of work, slip next st onto right-hand needle, take yarn under needle and back to original position, slip st back onto left-hand needle, then turn and proceed as instructed. This avoids holes in work.

**1ST ROW:** Knit to last 5 (5-6-6-6) sts, turn.

**2ND ROW:** Purl to last 5 (5-6-6-6) sts, turn.

**3RD ROW:** Knit to last 10 (10-12-12-12) sts, turn.

**4TH ROW:** Purl to last 10 (10-12-12-12) sts, turn.

**5TH ROW:** Knit to last 15 (15-18-18-18) sts, turn.

**6TH ROW:** Purl to last 15 (15-18-18-18) sts, turn.

**7TH ROW:** Knit to last 20 (20-24-24-25) sts, turn.

**8TH ROW:** Purl to last 20 (20-24-24-25) sts, turn.

**9TH ROW:** Knit to last 25 (25-29-30-32) sts, turn.

**10TH ROW:** Purl to last 25 (25-29-30-32) sts, turn.

**11TH ROW:** Knit to end.

**12TH ROW:** Purl across all sts to end.

**13TH ROW:** Purl.

**14TH ROW:** Knit.

**15TH ROW:** Purl.

**16TH ROW:** Purl.

Cast off loosely knitways.

## Neckband

Join shoulder seams. With right side facing, using set of 3.25mm needles and beg at left shoulder seam, knit up 76 (80-

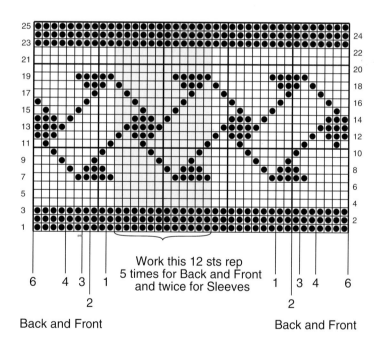

Work this 12 sts rep
5 times for Back and Front
and twice for Sleeves

6    4  3  1                                          1  3  4    6
        2                                                    2
Back and Front                                      Back and Front

**KEY**

☐ = Knit st on even numbered rows (right side) and purl st on odd numbered rows (wrong side).

◉ = Purl st on even numbered rows (right side) and knit st on odd numbered rows (wrong side).

**Note:** When working from Graph, read odd numbered rows (wrong side rows) from left to right and even numbered rows (right side rows) from right to left.

**For each row:** Beg at appropriate edge and work to beg of rep, work rep across as stated until number of sts after rep rem, then work these sts to end of row.

80-92-96) sts evenly around neck, incl sts
from stitch holders.
Purl 3 rounds.
**4TH ROUND:** * K2, P2, rep from * to end.
Rep 4th round 9 (9-11-11-15) times.
Purl 3 rounds.
Cast off very loosely knitways.

## To make up

Tie markers 14 (15-16-17-19) cm down
from beg of shoulder shaping on side
edges of Back and Front to mark armholes.
Sew in sleeves evenly between markers,
placing centres of sleeves to shoulder
seams.  Join side and sleeve seams.

# *Jumper with collar & matching hat*

## Measurements
Years

| 1 | 2 | 3 | 4 | 6 |
|---|---|---|---|---|

To fit chest (cm):

| 52.5 | 55 | 57.5 | 60 | 65 |
|---|---|---|---|---|

Actual measurement (cm):

| 60 | 64 | 67 | 70 | 77 |
|---|---|---|---|---|

Length (cm):

| 36 | 38 | 40 | 42 | 46 |
|---|---|---|---|---|

Sleeve length (cm):

| 19 | 21 | 23 | 26 | 31 |
|---|---|---|---|---|

## Materials

Cleckheaton Country 8 ply or Country
Naturals 8 ply (50g balls)
Jumper

| 5 | 6 | 6 | 7 | 7 |
|---|---|---|---|---|

Hat

| 1 | 1 | 1 | 2 | 2 |
|---|---|---|---|---|

or Cleckheaton Machinewash 8 ply or
Cleckheaton 8 ply Pure Wool (50g balls)
Jumper

| 5 | 6 | 7 | 7 | 8 |
|---|---|---|---|---|

Hat

| 1 | 1 | 1 | 2 | 2 |
|---|---|---|---|---|

One pair each 3.25mm and 4.00mm
knitting needles for Jumper and one set of
4.00mm knitting needles for Hat or the
required size to give correct tension; a
cable needle; knitter's needle for sewing
seams; 2 (2-3-3-3) buttons for Jumper.

## JUMPER

### Back
Using 4.00mm needles, cast on 68 (74-74-
80-86) sts.

BEGIN CABLE PATTERN
**1ST ROW:** P2, * K4, P2, rep from * to end.
**2ND ROW:** K2, * P4, K2, rep from * to end.
**3RD ROW:** P2, * C2F, P2, rep from * to
end.
**4TH ROW:** As 2nd row.
Last 4 rows form Cable Patt.
Work a further 8 (12-12-16-16) rows Cable
Patt, inc (dec-inc-dec-inc) one st in centre
of last row. 69 (73-75-79-87) sts.
Work in stocking st until work measures 19
(21-21-22-24) cm from beg, ending with a
purl row.

SHAPE RAGLAN ARMHOLES
Cast off 2 sts at beg of next 2 rows. 65 (69-
71-75-83) sts.

BEGIN RAGLAN PATTERN
**3RD ROW:** K1, C2B, sl1, K1, psso, knit to
last 7 sts, K2tog, C2F, K1. 63 (67-69-73-81)
sts.

TENSION
*These garments have
been designed at a
tension of 22 sts and 30
rows to 10cm over
stocking st, using
4.00mm needles.*

ABBREVIATIONS
*C2F = slip next 2 sts
onto cable needle and
leave at front of work,
K2, then K2 from cable
needle.
C2B = slip next 2 sts
onto cable needle and
leave at back of work,
K2, then K2 from cable
needle.*

*Guernsey-style jumpers
(page 52); Jumper with
collar & matching hat
(page 55); and
Patchwork jumper
(page 59).*

Shirts from Osh Kosh B'Gosh.
Riding hats, crop, gloves and
satchel from Bandanas, Charlton
Horseland. Pants and boots from
Thomas Cook Boot and Clothing
Co. Teddy from Teddy & Friends.

Work 3 rows stocking st, beg with purl row.
Last 4 rows form Cable Patt at raglan edge.
Rep last 4 rows 3 (3-4-4-3) times. 57 (61-
61-65-75) sts. **
Keeping Raglan Patt correct, dec one st
(inside 5 sts as before) at each end of next
and alt rows until 23 (25-25-27-27) sts rem.
Work 1 row.
Cast off rem sts loosely in patt.

## Front
Work as given for Back to **
Keeping Raglan Patt correct, dec one st
(inside 5 sts as before) at each end of next
and alt row/s until 53 (57-57-61-65) sts
rem.
Work 1 row.

DIVIDE FOR FRONT OPENING
**NEXT ROW:** Patt 5, sl1, K1, psso, K17 (19-
19-21-23), cast off next 5 sts, knit to last 7
sts, K2tog, patt 5.
Keeping Raglan Patt correct, cont on last
23 (25-25-27-29) sts and dec one st at
armhole edge (as before) in alt rows until
16 (18-18-19-20) sts rem.
Work 1 row.

sts and patt to end.
Keeping patt correct, cont on these 23 (25-25-27-29) sts and dec one st at armhole edge (as before) in alt rows until 15 (17-17-18-19) sts rem.

### SHAPE NECK
**NEXT ROW:** Cast off 3 (3-3-4-4) sts, patt to end. 12 (14-14-14-15) sts.
Dec one st at armhole edge (as before) in next and alt rows 5 (6-6-6-7) times in all, at same time dec one st at neck edge in 3rd (1st-1st-1st-3rd) row, then in foll 4th row/s 2 (3-3-3-3) times in all. 5 sts.
**NEXT ROW:** P5.
**NEXT ROW:** K1, (sl1, K1, psso) twice. 3 sts.
**NEXT ROW:** P3, turn. K3tog. Fasten off.

## Sleeves
Using 4.00mm needles, cast on 38 (38-44-44-44) sts.
Work 12 (16-16-20-20) rows Cable Patt as given for Back, dec 1 (1-3-1-1) st/s evenly in last row. 37 (37-41-43-43) sts.
Work 4 rows stocking st.
**5TH ROW:** K2, M1, knit to last 2 sts, M1, K2.
Cont inc one st (as before) at each end of foll 4th (alt-alt-alt-4th) rows until there are 51 (43-49-49-69) sts, then in foll 6th (4th-4th-4th-6th) row/s until there are 53 (57-65-69-73) sts.
Cont (without further inc) until work measures 19 (21-23-26-31) cm from beg, ending with a purl row.

### SHAPE RAGLAN
Cast off 2 sts at beg of next 2 rows. 49 (53-61-65-69) sts.

### BEGIN RAGLAN PATTERN
**3RD ROW:** K1, C2B, sl1, K1, psso, knit to last 7 sts, K2tog, C2F, K1. 47 (51-59-63-67) sts.
Work 3 rows st st, beg with a purl row.
Rep last 4 rows 7 (6-4-3-4) times. 33 (39-51-57-59) sts.
Keeping Raglan Patt correct, dec one st (inside 5 sts as before) at each end of next and alt rows until 15 sts rem.
Work 1 row.
Cast off loosely in patt.

### SHAPE NECK
**NEXT ROW:** Cast off 3 (3-3-4-4) sts, patt to last 7 sts, K2tog, patt 5. 12 (14-14-14-15) sts.
Dec one st at armhole edge (as before) in alt rows 5 (6-6-6-7) times, at same time dec one st at neck edge in 4th (2nd-2nd-2nd-4th) row, then in foll 4th row/s 2 (3-3-3-3) times in all. 5 sts.
**NEXT ROW:** P5.
**NEXT ROW:** (K2tog) twice, K1. 3 sts.
**NEXT ROW:** P3, turn. K3tog. Fasten off.
With wrong side facing, join yarn to rem

## Left front band

(If making for girl, omit buttonholes)
Using 3.25mm needles, cast on 8 sts.
**1st Row:** K2, P1, K1, P1, K3.
**2nd Row:** P3, (K1, P1) twice, K1.
Rep 1st and 2nd rows 2 (2-1-1-2) time/s.
**\*\*Buttonhole Row:** K2, P1, K2tog, yfwd, K3.
Rep 2nd row once, then 1st and 2nd rows 3 (3-2-2-2) times. \*\*
Rep from \*\* to \*\* 0 (0-1-1-1) time/s, then rep buttonhole row once. 2 (2-3-3-3) buttonholes in all.
Rep 2nd row once, then 1st and 2nd rows once.
Cast off loosely in rib patt.

## Right front band

(If making for boy, omit buttonholes)
Using 3.25mm needles, cast on 8 sts.
**1st Row:** K3, P1, K1, P1, K2.
**2nd Row:** K1, (P1, K1) twice, P3.
Rep 1st and 2nd rows 2 (2-1-1-2) time/s.
**\*\*\*Buttonhole Row:** K3, yfwd, K2tog, P1, K2.
Rep 2nd row once, then 1st and 2nd rows 3 (3-2-2-2) times. \*\*\*
Rep from \*\*\* to \*\*\* 0 (0-1-1-1) time/s, then rep buttonhole row once. 2 (2-3-3-3) buttonholes in all.
Rep 2nd row once, then 1st and 2nd rows once.
Cast off loosely in rib patt.

## Collar

Using 4.00mm needles, cast on 122 (128-128-134-140) sts.
Work 11 (15-15-19-19) rows Cable Patt as given for Back.
**Next Row:** K2, P3, * P2tog, P2tog tbl, P2, rep from * to last 3 sts, P1, K2. 84 (88-88-92-96) sts.
Cast off.

## To make up

Join raglan seams, noting that tops of sleeves form part of neckline. Join side and sleeve seams. Sew front bands in position, placing ribbed edge to garment and crossing buttonhole band over other band. Using a flat seam, sew cast-off edge of collar evenly in position, beg and ending at centre of front bands.
Sew on buttons.

# HAT

Using set of 4.00mm needles, cast on 84 (90-90-96-96) sts.
Divide sts so that there are 28 (30-30-32-32) sts on each needle.

Begin Cable Pattern
**1st Round:** * P2, K4, rep from * to end.
Rep 1st round once.
**3rd Round:** * P2, C2F, rep from * to end.
Rep 1st round once.
Rep last 4 rounds 1 (2-2-3-3) time/s, dec 0 (6-6-8-8) sts evenly in last round. 84 (84-84-88-88) sts [8 (12-12-16-16) rounds Cable Patt in all].
**Next Round:** * Inc in next st, K1, rep from * to end. 126 (126-126-132-132) sts.
Divide sts so that there are 42 (42-42-44-44) sts on each needle.
**Next Round:** Knit.
Rep last round 17 (19-19-21-21) times.
**Next Round:** K6 (0-0-6-6), * K2tog, K3 (5-5-5-5), rep from * to end. 102 (108-108-114-114) sts.
Divide sts so that there are 34 (36-36-38-38) sts on each needle.

Shape Crown
**1st Round:** * K8, sl1, K2tog, psso, K6 (7-7-8-8), rep from * to end. 90 (96-96-102-102) sts.
**2nd and Alt Rounds:** Knit.
**3rd Round:** * K7, sl1, K2tog, psso, K5 (6-6-7-7), rep from * to end. 78 (84-84-90-90) sts.
**5th Round:** * K6, sl1, K2tog, psso, K4 (5-5-6-6), rep from * to end. 66 (72-72-78-78) sts.
**7th Round:** * K5, sl1, K2tog, psso, K3 (4-4-5-5), rep from * to end. 54 (60-60-66-66) sts.
Cont dec in this manner in alt rounds until 18 (12-12-18-18) sts rem.
Break off yarn, run end through rem sts, draw up and fasten off securely.

# Patchwork jumper

## Measurements

| Years | | | | |
|---|---|---|---|---|
| 1 | 2 | 3 | 4 | 6 |

To fit chest (cm):

| | | | | |
|---|---|---|---|---|
| 52.5 | 55 | 57.5 | 60 | 65 |

cm

Actual measurement (approx) (cm):

| | | | | |
|---|---|---|---|---|
| 60 | 64 | 67 | 70 | 77 |

Length (approx) (cm):

| | | | | |
|---|---|---|---|---|
| 34 | 35 | 40 | 41 | 48 |

Sleeve length (cm):

| | | | | |
|---|---|---|---|---|
| 21 | 23 | 25 | 28 | 33 |

## Materials

Cleckheaton Country 8 ply or Country Naturals 8 ply (50g balls)

1st Contrast (C1):

| | | | | |
|---|---|---|---|---|
| 2 | 2 | 3 | 3 | 3 |

2nd Contrast (C2):

| | | | | |
|---|---|---|---|---|
| 3 | 3 | 3 | 4 | 4 |

3rd Contrast (C3):

| | | | | |
|---|---|---|---|---|
| 2 | 2 | 3 | 3 | 3 |

4th Contrast (C4):

| | | | | |
|---|---|---|---|---|
| 2 | 2 | 2 | 3 | 3 |

5th Contrast (C5):

| | | | | |
|---|---|---|---|---|
| 2 | 2 | 2 | 3 | 3 |

or Cleckheaton Machinewash 8 ply or Cleckheaton 8 ply Pure Wool (50 g balls)

1st Contrast (C1):

| | | | | |
|---|---|---|---|---|
| 1 | 1 | 2 | 2 | 2 |

2nd Contrast (C2):

| | | | | |
|---|---|---|---|---|
| 2 | 2 | 2 | 3 | 3 |

3rd Contrast (C3):

| | | | | |
|---|---|---|---|---|
| 1 | 1 | 2 | 2 | 2 |

4th Contrast (C4):

| | | | | |
|---|---|---|---|---|
| 1 | 1 | 2 | 2 | 2 |

5th Contrast (C5):

| | | | | |
|---|---|---|---|---|
| 1 | 1 | 1 | 2 | 2 |

One pair each 3.25mm and 4.00mm knitting needles or the required size to give correct tension; 2 stitch holders; knitter's needle for sewing seams; Sizes 1, 2 and 3 only-3 buttons for shoulder opening.

## Back

Using 3.25mm needles and C1, cast on 66 (70-74-78-82) sts.

**1st Row:** K2, * P2, K2, rep from * to end.
**2nd Row:** P2, * K2, P2, rep from * to end.
**3rd Row:** Using C2, knit.
**4th Row:** As 2nd row.

Rep 3rd and 4th rows 4 times, in stripes of 2 rows C3, 2 rows C4, 2 rows C5 and 2 rows C1.

Last 10 rows form rib patt.

Work a further 2 (6-6-8-8) rows rib patt, inc 6 (4-6-4-8) sts evenly across last row. 72 (74-80-82-90) sts [14 (18-18-20-20) rows rib in all].

Change to 4.00mm needles.

BEGIN 1ST PATTERN
(see **NOTE** at right)
**1st Row:** K18 (19-20-21-23) C1, K18 (18-20-20-22) C2, K18 (18-20-20-22) C3, K18 (19-20-21-23) C4.
**2nd Row:** P18 (19-20-21-23) C4, work 2nd

**TENSION**

*This garment has been designed at a tension of 22 sts and 30 rows to 10cm over stocking st, using 4.00mm needles, and 23 sts and 36 rows to 10cm over double moss st patt, using 4.00mm needles.*

**NOTE:** *When changing colours in centre of row, twist the colour to be used underneath and to the right of colour just used, making sure both yarns are worked firmly at joins. Always change colours on wrong side of work so colour change does not show on right side. Use a separate ball of yarn for each section of colour.*

row of Graph across next 18 (18-20-20-22) sts using C3, P18 (18-20-20-22) C2, work 2nd row of Graph across next 18 (18-20-20-22) sts using C1, P0 (1-0-1-1) C1.

**3RD ROW:** K0 (1-0-1-1) C1, work 3rd row of Graph using C1, K18 (18-20-20-22) C2, work 3rd row of Graph using C3, K18 (19-20-21-23) C4.

**4TH ROW:** P18 (19-20-21-23) C4, work 4th row of Graph using C3, P18 (18-20-20-22) C2, work 4th row of Graph using C1, P0 (1-0-1-1) C1.

**5TH ROW:** K0 (1-0-1-1) C1, work 5th row of Graph using C1, K18 (18-20-20-22) C2, work 5th row of Graph using C3, K18 (19-20-21-23) C4.

Rows 2 to 5 incl form patt for stocking st and double moss st squares.

Work a further 21 (21-25-25-31) rows patt. Last 26 (26-30-30-36) rows form 1st Patt.

BEGIN 2ND PATTERN

**1ST ROW:** K18 (19-20-21-23) C3, K18 (18-20-20-22) C4, K18 (18-20-20-22) C5, K18 (19-20-21-23) C2.

**2ND ROW:** P0 (1-0-1-1) C2, work 2nd row of Graph across next 18 (18-20-20-22) sts using C2, P18 (18-20-20-22) C5, work 2nd row of Graph across next 18 (18-20-20-22) sts using C4, P18 (19-20-21-23) C3.

**3RD ROW:** K18 (19-20-21-23) C3, work 3rd row of Graph using C4, K18 (18-20-20-22) C5, work 3rd row of Graph using C2, K0 (1-0-1-1) C2.

**4TH ROW:** As 2nd row, working 4th row of Graph.

**5TH ROW:** As 3rd row, working 5th row of Graph.

Rows 2 to 5 incl form patt for stocking st and double moss st squares.

Work a further 21 (21-25-25-31) rows patt. Last 26 (26-30-30-36) rows form 2nd Patt.

BEGIN 3RD PATTERN

Work 26 (26-30-30-36) rows of 1st Patt, working C4 in place of C1, C1 in place of C2, C2 in place of C3 and C3 in place of C4. **

BEGIN 4TH PATTERN

Work 24 (24-28-28-34) rows 2nd Patt, working C2 in place of C3, C5 in place of C4, C4 in place of C5 and C1 in place of C2.

SHAPE SHOULDERS

Keeping 4th Patt correct for rem, cast off 8 (8-9-9-10) sts at beg of next 4 rows, then 7 (7-8-8-10) sts at beg of foll 2 rows.

Leave rem 26 (28-28-30-30) sts on a stitch holder.

## Front

Work as given for Back to **.

BEGIN 4TH PATTERN

Work 8 (8-12-10-16) rows 4th Patt as given for Back.

SHAPE NECK

Keeping 4th Patt correct for rem.

**NEXT ROW:** Patt 29 (30-33-34-38), turn.

Cont on these 29 (30-33-34-38) sts and dec one st at neck edge in every row until 27 (26-29-32-36) sts rem, then in alt row/s until 25 (25-28-26-30) sts rem.

Work 1 (1-1-3-3) row/s patt.

SHAPE SHOULDER

**NOTE:** There are 8 rows less than Back to beg of shoulder shaping on this side of Front only to allow for shoulder band on first 3 sizes only.

Cast off 8 (8-9-9-10) sts at beg of next row and foll alt row. Sizes 1, 2 and 3 only: at same time dec one st at neck edge in 1st row and foll alt row.

All sizes: work 1 row. Cast off rem 7 (7-8-8-10) sts.

Slip next 14 sts onto stitch holder and leave. With right side facing, join yarn to rem sts and patt to end.

Cont on these 29 (30-33-34-38) sts and dec one st at neck edge in every row until 27 (26-29-32-36) sts rem, then in alt rows until 23 (23-26-26-30) sts rem.

Work 6 (6-6-4-4) rows patt.

SHAPE SHOULDER

Cast off 8 (8-9-9-10) sts at beg of next row and foll alt row.

Work 1 row. Cast off rem 7 (7-8-8-10) sts.

## Sleeves

Using 3.25mm needles and C1, cast on 34 (34-34-38-38) sts.

Work 13 (17-17-19-19) rows rib patt as given for Back.

**NEXT ROW (WRONG SIDE):** Rib 2 (3-4-6-2), * inc in next st, rib 3 (2-1-2-2) rep from * to last 0 (1-2-2-0) st/s, rib 0 (1-2-2-0). 42 (44-48-48-50) sts.
Change to 4.00mm needles.

BEGIN 1ST PATTERN
**1ST ROW:** K3 (4-4-4-3) C1, K18 (18-20-20-22) C2, K18 (18-20-20-22) C3, K3 (4-4-4-3) C4.
**2ND ROW:** P3 (4-4-4-3) C4, work 2nd row of Graph across next 18 (18-20-20-22) sts using C3, P18 (18-20-20-22) C2, using C1-[K0 (0-2-2-0), P2, K1 (2-0-0-1) ].
**3RD ROW:** Using C1-[K1 (2-0-0-1), P2, K0 (0-2-2-0)], K18 (18-20-20-22) C2, work 3rd row of Graph using C3, K3 (4-4-4-3) C4.
**4TH ROW :** P3 (4-4-4-3) C4, work 4th row of Graph using C3, P18 (18-20-20-22) C2, using C1-[P0 (0-2-2-0), K2, P1 (2-0-0-1)].
Keeping patt correct as for Back, as placed in last 4 rows and noting to work extra sts into appropriate patt at sides, inc one st at each end of next and alt rows until there are 52 (50-60-58-56) sts, then in foll 4th rows until there are 68 (70-80-82-90) sts.
Cont in patt (without further inc) until work measures 21 (23-25-28-33) cm from beg, working last row on wrong side.

SHAPE TOP
Keeping patt correct, cast off 5 (5-6-6-7) sts at beg of next 8 rows, then 6 (6-7-7-7) sts at beg of foll 2 rows.
Cast off rem 16 (18-18-20-20) sts.

## Neckband
Join right shoulder seam. With right side facing, using 3.25mm needles and C5, knit up 8 (9-9-19-19) sts evenly along left side of front neck, knit across sts from front stitch holder, knit up 14 (15-15-19-19) sts evenly along right side of front neck, then knit across sts from back stitch holder. 62 (66-66-82-82) sts.
Work 9 rows rib patt as given for Back, beg with a 4th row and working in stripes of 1 row C5, 2 rows C4, 2 rows C3, 2 rows C2 and 2 rows C1.
Using C1, cast off loosely in rib.

## Front shoulder band
(Sizes 1, 2 and 3 only)

With right side facing, using 3.25mm needles and C5, knit up 34 (34-38) sts evenly along left shoulder and across end of neckband.
Work 3 rows rib patt as given for Back, beg with a 4th row and working in stripes of 1 row C5 and 2 rows C4.
**NEXT ROW:** Using C3, K10, cast off 2 sts, [K8 (8-10), cast off 2 sts] twice, K2.
**NEXT ROW:** Rib 2, cast on 2 sts, [rib 8 (8-10), cast on 2 sts] twice, rib 10. 3 buttonholes.
Work a further 4 rows rib patt in stripes of 2 rows C2 and 2 rows C1.
Using C1, cast off loosely in rib.

## Back shoulder band
(Sizes 1, 2 and 3 only)
Work to correspond with Front shoulder Band, omitting buttonholes. Place front shoulder band over back shoulder band and oversew ends of bands tog at armhole edge. Sew on buttons.

## To make up
Sizes 4 and 6 only: join left shoulder and neckband seam.
All sizes: tie markers 14 (15-16-17-19) cm down from beg of shoulder shaping (or top of front shoulder band) on side edges of Back and Front to mark armholes. Sew in sleeves evenly between markers, placing centres of sleeves to shoulder seams (or top front shoulder band). Join side and sleeve seams.

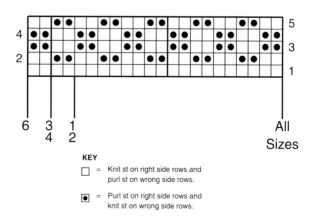

KEY
☐ = Knit st on right side rows and purl st on wrong side rows.
⊡ = Purl st on right side rows and knit st on wrong side rows.

NOTE: Read odd numbered rows (right side rows) from right to left and even numbered rows (wrong side rows) from left to right.

*Country Casuals*

# Jumper with teddy & checks

**TENSION**

*This garment has been designed at a tension of 22 sts and 30 rows to 10cm over stocking st, using 4.00mm needles and 23 sts and 36 rows to 10cm over Double Moss St, using 4.00mm needles.*

## Measurements

Years

| 1 | 2 | 3 | 4 | 6 |
|---|---|---|---|---|

To fit chest (cm):

| 52.5 | 55 | 57.5 | 60 | 65 |
|---|---|---|---|---|

Actual measurement (approx) (cm):

| 60 | 64 | 67 | 70 | 77 |
|---|---|---|---|---|

Length (approx) (cm):

| 36 | 38 | 40 | 42 | 46 |
|---|---|---|---|---|

Sleeve length (cm):

| 21 | 23 | 25 | 28 | 33 |
|---|---|---|---|---|

## Materials

Cleckheaton Country 8 ply or Country Naturals 8 ply (50g balls)

Main Colour (MC):

| 7 | 7 | 8 | 9 | 10 |
|---|---|---|---|---|

1st Contrast (C1):

| 1 | 1 | 1 | 1 | 1 |
|---|---|---|---|---|

2nd Contrast (C2):

| 1 | 1 | 1 | 1 | 1 |
|---|---|---|---|---|

or Cleckheaton Machinewash 8 ply or Cleckheaton 8 ply Pure Wool (50g balls)

Main Colour (MC):

| 6 | 7 | 7 | 8 | 9 |
|---|---|---|---|---|

1st Contrast (C1):

| 1 | 1 | 1 | 1 | 1 |
|---|---|---|---|---|

2nd Contrast (C2):

| 1 | 1 | 1 | 1 | 1 |
|---|---|---|---|---|

One pair each 3.25mm and 4.00mm knitting needles or the required size to give correct tension; 2 stitch holders; DMC stranded cotton for Teddy's face (see Graph for shades and quantities); knitter's needle for sewing seams and embroidery; 6 buttons.

## Front

Using 3.25mm needles and MC, cast on 66 (70-74-74-82) sts.

**1ST ROW:** K2, * P2, K2, rep from * to end.

**2ND ROW:** P2, * K2, P2, rep from * to end.

Rep 1st and 2nd rows 4 (5-5-7-7) times, then 1st row once.

**NEXT ROW (WRONG SIDE):** Rib 6 (10-8-8-9), * inc in next st, rib 9 (9-10-7-8), rep from * to last 0 (0-0-2-1) st/s, rib 0 (0-0-2-1). 72 (76-80-82-90) sts [12 (14-14-18-18) rows rib in all].

Change to 4.00mm needles

**1ST ROW:** P0 (1-0-0-0), K1 (2-1-2-2), * P2, K2, rep from * to last 3 (1-3-0-0) st/s, P2 (1-2-0-0), K1 (0-1-0-0).

**2ND ROW:** K0 (1-0-0-0), P1 (2-1-2-2), * K2, P2, rep from * to last 3 (1-3-0-0) st/s, K2 (1-2-0-0), P1 (0-1-0-0).

**3RD ROW:** As 2nd row.

**4TH ROW:** As 1st row.

Last 4 rows form Double Moss St.

Cont in Double Moss St until work measures approx 15 (16-17-18-20) cm from beg, ending with a 4th patt row.

PLACE CHECK PATTERN
(see side **NOTE** on page 65)

**1ST ROW:** Patt 17 (19-21-22-26), K11, K2tog, K12, K2tog, K11, patt 17 (19-21-22-26). 70 (74-78-80-88) sts.

**2ND ROW:** Patt 17 (19-21-22-26), P36, patt 17 (19-21-22-26).

**3RD ROW:** Patt 17 (19-21-22-26), K36, patt 17 (19-21-22-26).

**4TH ROW:** As 2nd row.

**5TH ROW:** Patt 17 (19-21-22-26) MC, K36C1, patt 17 (19-21-22-26) MC.

**6TH ROW:** Patt 17 (19-21-22-26) MC, P36C1, patt 17 (19-21-22-26) MC.

**7TH ROW:** As 5th row.

**8TH ROW:** As 6th row.

**9TH ROW:** Using MC, K13 (15-17-18-22), K2tog, K40, K2tog, K13 (15-17-18-22). 68 (72-76-78-86) sts.

Work rows 10 to 32 incl from Graph, working Check detail at sides in stripes (as before).

**33RD ROW:** Using MC, K13 (15-17-18-22), inc in next st, K40, inc in next st, K13 (15-17-18-22). 70 (74-78-80-88) sts.

**34TH ROW:** K0 (1-0-0-0), P1 (2-1-2-2), (K2, P2) 4 (4-5-5-6) times, P36, (P2, K2) 4 (4-5-5-6) times, P1 (2-1-2-2), K0 (1-0-0-0).

**35TH ROW:** K0 (1-0-0-0), P1 (2-1-2-2), (K2, P2) 4 (4-5-5-6) times, K36, (P2, K2) 4 (4-5-5-6) times, P1 (2-1-2-2), K0 (1-0-0-0).

**36TH ROW:** P0 (1-0-0-0), K1 (2-1-2-2), (P2, K2) 4 (4-5-5-6) times, P36, (K2, P2) 4 (4-5-5-6) times, K1 (2-1-2-2), P0 (1-0-0-0).

Keeping Double Moss St for 17 (19-21-22-26) sts at each end correct as placed in last 3 rows, work rows 5 to 8 incl once.

**41ST ROW:** Using MC for rem, Patt 17 (19-21-22-26), K11, inc in next st, K12, inc in next st, K11, patt 17 (19-21-22-26). 72 (76-80-82-90) sts. **

Working in Double Moss St across all sts for rem, work 13 (13-17-21-25) rows patt.

SHAPE NECK

**NEXT ROW:** Patt 29 (31-32-33-37), turn.
Keeping patt correct, cont on these 29 (31-32-33-37) sts and dec one st at neck edge in every row until 24 (25-26-27-31) sts rem. Sizes 4 and 6 only: then in alt row/s until (26-29) sts rem.
All sizes: work 0 (1-1-1-1) row/s.

SHAPE SHOULDER

**NOTE:** There will be 8 rows less on Front than on Back to beg of shoulder shaping to allow for shoulder bands.

Cast off 7 (8-8-8-9) sts at beg of next row and foll alt row, at same time dec one st at neck edge in first and foll alt row.
Work 1 row. Cast off rem 8 (7-8-8-9) sts.
Slip next 14 (14-16-16-16) sts onto a stitch holder and leave. With right side facing, join MC to rem sts and patt to end.
Cont on these 29 (31-32-33-37) sts.
Keeping patt correct, dec one st at neck edge in every row until 23 (25-26-27-31) sts rem. Sizes 2, 3, 4, and 6 only: then in alt row/s until (24-25-25-28) sts rem.
All sizes:

SHAPE SHOULDER

Cast off 7 (8-8-8-9) sts at beg of next row and foll alt row, at same time dec one st at neck edge in 2nd row.
Work 1 row. Cast off rem 8 (7-8-8-9) sts.

## Back

Work as given for Front to **, omitting MC background for Teddy's face and working this section entirely in stripes for check embroidery on completion of knitting.
Work in Double Moss across all sts for rem and work 27 (29-33-39-45) rows patt.

SHAPE SHOULDERS

Keeping patt correct, cast off 7 (8-8-8-9) sts at beg of next 4 rows, then 8 (7-8-8-9) sts at beg of foll 2 rows.
Leave rem 28 (30-32-34-36) sts on stitch holder.

## Sleeves

Using 3.25mm needles and MC, cast on 34 (34-38-42-42) sts.
Work 11 (13-13-17-17) rows rib as given for Back.

**NEXT ROW (WRONG SIDE):** Rib 3 (0-1-3-3), * inc in next st, rib 2 (2-3-3-3), rep from * to last 4 (1-1-3-3) st/s, inc in next st, rib 3 (0-0-2-2). 44 (46-48-52-52) sts.
Change to 4.00mm needles.

**1ST ROW:** K1 (0-1-1-1), P2, * K2, P2, rep from * to last 1 (0-1-1-1) st/s, K1 (0-1-1-1).

**2ND ROW:** P1 (0-1-1-1), K2, * P2, K2, rep from * to last 1 (0-1-1-1) st/s, P1 (0-1-1-1).

**3RD ROW:** As 2nd row.

**4TH ROW:** As 1st row.

**NOTE:** *Work all Teddy detail in MC. The checks are knitted as stocking st stripes of 4 rows each MC and C1. On completion of knitting the C1 and C2 detail is added to the MC and C1 stripes respectively as indicated on Graph, using Knitting St Embroidery. When changing colours in centre of row, twist the colour to be used underneath and to the right of colour just used, making sure both yarns are worked firmly at joins. Always change colours on wrong side of work so colour change does not show on right side. Use a separate ball of yarn for each section of colour. Teddy's face is embroidered using Knitting St Embroidery on completion of knitting.*

Last 4 rows form Double Moss St.
Keeping Double Moss St correct and noting to work extra sts into Double Moss St, inc one st at each end of next and foll alt (alt-4th-4th-4th) row/s until there are 48 (50-76-80-92) sts, then in foll 4th (4th-6th-6th-6th) row/s until there are 70 (74-78-84-94) sts.
Cont in Double Moss St (without further inc) until work measures 21 (23-25-28-33) cm from beg, working last row on wrong side.

SHAPE TOP
Cast off 5 (6-6-6-7) sts at beg of next 6 (8-8-6-6) rows, then 6 (5-6-7-8) sts at beg of foll 4 (2-2-4-4) rows.
Cast off rem 16 (16-18-20-20) sts in patt.

## Back neck and shoulder band

With right side facing, using 3.25mm needles and MC, knit up 24 (25-26-26-29) sts evenly across first shoulder, knit across sts on stitch holder - inc 0 (0-0-2-2) sts, then knit up 24 (25-26-26-29) sts evenly across second shoulder. 76 (80-84-88-96) sts.
**1st Row:** P3, * K2, P2, rep from * to last st, P1.
**2nd Row:** K3, * P2, K2, rep from * to last st, K1.
Rep 1st and 2nd rows 3 times, then 1st row once.
Cast off loosely in rib.

## Front neck and shoulder band

With right side facing, using 3.25mm needles and MC, knit up 24 (25-26-26-29) sts evenly across first shoulder, 9 (10-12-14-15) sts evenly along left side of neck, knit across sts on stitch holder, knit up 9 (10-12-14-15) sts evenly along right side of neck, then 24 (25-26-26-29) sts evenly across second shoulder. 80 (84-92-96-104) sts.
Work 3 rows rib as for Back Neck and Shoulder Band.
**4TH ROW:** Rib 5 (5-7-7-5), * cast off 2 sts, rib 6 (6-6-6-8) *, rep from * to * twice, rib to last 23 (23-25-25-27) sts, rep from * to * twice, cast off 2 sts, rib 5 (5-7-7-5).
**5TH ROW:** Rib 5 (5-7-7-5) * cast on 2 sts, rib 6 (6-6-6-8) *, rep from * to * twice, rib to last 17 (17-17-19-21) sts, rep from * to * twice, cast on 2 sts, rib 5 (5-7-7-5). 6 buttonholes.
Work 4 rows rib.
Cast off loosely in rib.

## To make up

Embroider C1 and C2 check detail from graph to Back (fill completely) and Front. Using DMC stranded cotton double, embroider Teddy's face from graph to Front.
Place front neck and shoulder band over back neck and shoulder and over sew ends of bands tog at armhole edge. Tie markers 15 (15.5-16.5-17-20) cm down from shoulder (top of front band) to mark armholes. Sew in sleeves evenly between markers, placing centres of sleeves to shoulder seams. Join side and sleeves seam. Sew on buttons.

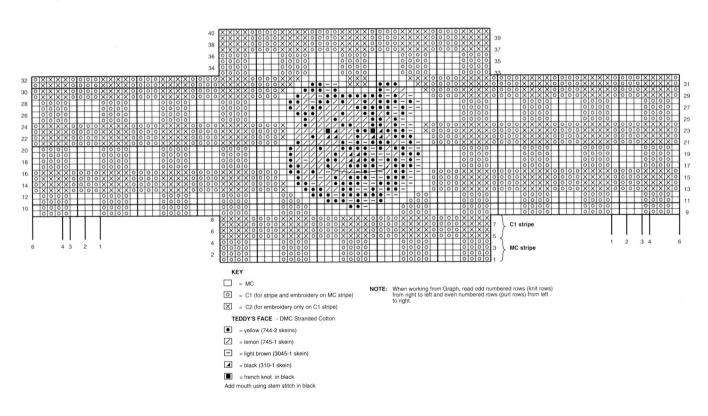

**KEY**

☐ = MC

◎ = C1 (for stripe and embroidery on MC stripe)

☒ = C2 (for embroidery only on C1 stripe)

**TEDDY'S FACE** - DMC Stranded Cotton

● = yellow (744-2 skeins)

⟋ = lemon (745-1 skein)

— = light brown (3045-1 skein)

◢ = black (310-1 skein)

■ = french knot in black

Add mouth using stem stitch in black

NOTE: When working from Graph, read odd numbered rows (knit rows) from right to left and even numbered rows (purl rows) from left to right.

# *Aran jumper & hat*

## Measurements

| Years | | | | |
|---|---|---|---|---|
| 1 | 2 | 3 | 4 | 6 |

**Jumper**
To fit chest (cm):

| | | | | |
|---|---|---|---|---|
| 52.5 | 55 | 57.5 | 60 | 65 |

Actual measurement (approx) (cm):

| | | | | |
|---|---|---|---|---|
| 60 | 64 | 68 | 70 | 77 |

Length (cm):

| | | | | |
|---|---|---|---|---|
| 36 | 38 | 40 | 42 | 46 |

Sleeve length (cm):

| | | | | |
|---|---|---|---|---|
| 21 | 23 | 25 | 28 | 33 |

**Hat**
To fit head (approx) (cm):

| | | | | |
|---|---|---|---|---|
| 49 | 51 | 51 | 52 | 53 |

Finished length (cm):

| | | | | |
|---|---|---|---|---|
| 14 | 15 | 16 | 16 | 17 |

## Materials

Cleckheaton Country 8 ply or Country Naturals 8 ply or Cleckheaton Machinewash 8 ply or Cleckheaton 8 ply Pure Wool (50g balls)

Jumper

| | | | | |
|---|---|---|---|---|
| 7 | 7 | 8 | 8 | 9 |

Hat

| | | | | |
|---|---|---|---|---|
| 1 | 1 | 2 | 2 | 2 |

One pair each 3.25mm and 4.00mm knitting needles or the required size to give correct tension; a cable needle; 2 stitch holders for Jumper; Sizes 1, 2 and 3 only - 3 buttons for shoulder opening; knitter's needle for sewing seams.

## JUMPER

### Back

Using 3.25mm needles, cast on 66 (70-74-78-86) sts.

**1st Row:** K2, * P2, K2, rep from * to end.
**2nd Row:** P2, * K2, P2, rep from * to end.
Rep 1st and 2nd rows 5 (5-5-7-8) times, then 1st row once.
**Next Row (wrong side):** Rib 6 (2-6-10-14), * inc in next st, rib 3, rep from * to last 0 (0-0-8-12) sts, rib 0 (0-0-8-12). 81 (87-91-93-101) sts [14 (14-14-18-20) rows rib in all].
Change to 4.00mm needles and Beg Patt:
**1st Row:** K2 (1-3-0-0), (P1, K3) 3 (4-4-5-6) times, P1, K2, work 1st row of Graph over next 47 sts, K2, P1, (K3, P1) 3 (4-4-5-6) times, K2 (1-3-0-0).
**2nd Row:** P17 (20-22-23-27), work 2nd row of Graph, P17 (20-22-23-27).
**3rd Row:** K0 (3-1-2-2), (P1, K3) 4 (4-5-5-6) times, K1, work 3rd row of Graph, K1, (K3, P1) 4 (4-5-5-6) times, K0 (3-1-2-2).
**4th Row:** P17 (20-22-23-27), work 4th row of Graph, P17 (20-22-23-27).
**5th Row:** As 1st row, working 5th row of Graph.
**6th Row:** As 2nd row, working 6th row of Graph.
**7th Row:** As 3rd row, working 7th row of Graph.
**8th Row:** As 4th row, working 8th row of Graph.
Last 8 rows form patt.

## TENSION
*These garments have been designed at a tension of 22 sts and 30 rows to 10cm over stocking st, using 4.00mm needles.*

*Teddy's waistcoat (page 46); Teddy's Fair Isle cardigan & scarf (page 71); Jumper with teddy & checks (page 64); and Aran jumper & hat (page 67).*

*Shirts, jeans and bandana from Osh Kosh B'Gosh. Boots from Thomas Cook Boot and Clothing Co. Teddy cart from the Teddy Bear Shop. Teddies from The Teddy Bear Shop and Teddy & Friends.*

Cont in patt until work measures 35 (37-39-41-45) cm from beg, working last row on wrong side.

SHAPE SHOULDERS
Keeping patt correct, cast off 8 (9-10-10-11) sts at beg of next 4 rows, then 9 (9-9-9-10) sts at beg of foll 2 rows.
Leave rem 31 (33-33-35-37) sts on a stitch holder.

## Front
Work as given for Back until there are 12 (14-14-16-16) rows less than Back to beg of shoulder shaping, thus working last row on wrong side.

SHAPE NECK
NEXT ROW: Patt 32 (35-37-38-41), turn. Keeping patt correct cont on these 32 (35-37-38-41) sts, and dec one st at neck edge in every row until 27 (29-31-34-37) sts rem.
Sizes 4 and 6 only: then in alt rows until (29-32) sts rem.
All sizes: work 0 (1-1-1-1) row/s.

## SHAPE SHOULDER

**NOTE:** There are 6 rows less than Back to beg of shoulder shaping on this side of Front only to allow for shoulder band on first 3 sizes only.

Cast off 8 (9-10-10-11) sts at beg of next row and foll alt row. Sizes 1, 2 and 3 only: at same time dec one st at neck edge in first row and foll alt row.
All sizes: work 1 row. Cast off rem 9 (9-9-9-10) sts.
Slip next 17 (17-17-17-19) sts onto stitch holder and leave. With right side facing, join yarn to rem sts and patt to end.
Keeping patt correct, cont on these 32 (35-37-38-41) sts and dec one st at neck edge in every row until 26 (29-31-34-37) sts rem, then in alt rows until 25 (27-29-29-32) sts rem.
Work 4 (4-4-2-2) rows.

## SHAPE SHOULDER

Cast off 8 (9-10-10-11) sts at beg of next row and foll alt row.
Work 1 row. Cast off rem 9 (9-9-9-10) sts.

## Sleeves

Using 3.25mm needles, cast on 34 (34-38-38-38) sts.
Work 13 (13-13-17-19) rows rib as given for Back.
**NEXT ROW (WRONG SIDE):** Rib 6 (6-10-6-6), inc once in each st to last 5 (5-5-7-5) sts, rib 5 (5-5-7-5). 57 (57-61-63-65) sts.
Change to 4.00mm needles and Beg Patt:
**1ST ROW:** K2 (2-0-1-2), (P1, K3) 0 (0-1-1-1) time/s, P1, K2, Work 1st row of Graph across next 47 sts, K2, P1, (K3, P1) 0 (0-1-1-1) time/s, K2 (2-0-1-2).
**2ND ROW:** P5 (5-7-8-9), work 2nd row of Graph, P5 (5-7-8-9).
**3RD ROW:** K0 (0-2-3-0), (P1, K3) 1 (1-1-1-2) time/s, K1, work 3rd row of Graph, K1, (K3, P1) 1 (1-1-1-2) time/s, K0 (0-2-3-0).
**4TH ROW:** P5 (5-7-8-9), work 4th row of Graph, P5 (5-7-8-9).
Cont in patt as given for Back as placed in last 4 rows and noting to work extra sts into side patt, inc one st at each end of next and foll alt (alt-alt-4th-4th) rows until there are 63 (65-67-89-97) sts, then in foll 4th

(4th-4th-6th-6th) row/s until there are 79 (83-89-91-99) sts.
Cont (without further inc) until work measures 21 (23-25-28-33) cm from beg, working last row on wrong side.

## SHAPE TOP

Keeping patt correct, cast off 6 (6-7-7-7) sts at beg of next 8 rows, then 6 (7-6-6-9) sts at beg of foll 2 rows.
Cast off rem 19 (21-21-23-25) sts.

## Neckband

Join right shoulder seam. With right side facing and using 3.25mm needles, knit up 10 (11-11-19-19) sts evenly along left side of front neck, knit across sts from stitch holder-dec 2 sts evenly across, knit up 16 (17-17-19-19) sts evenly along right side of neck, then knit across sts from back stitch holder- dec 6 sts evenly across. 66 (70-70-82-86) sts.
Work 5cm rib as given for Back, beg and ending with a 2nd row.
Cast off loosely in rib.

## Front shoulder band

(Sizes 1, 2 and 3 only)
Fold neckband in half onto wrong side and slip stitch loosely in position. With right side facing and using 3.25mm needles, knit up 34 (34-38) sts evenly along left shoulder and across end of neckband, working through both thickness.
Work 2 rows rib as given for Back, beg with a 2nd row.
**NEXT ROW:** Rib 2, cast off 2 sts, [rib 8 (8-10), cast off 2 sts] twice, rib 10.
**NEXT ROW:** Rib 10, cast on 2 sts, [rib 8 (8-10), cast on 2 sts] twice, rib 2. 3 buttonholes.
Work 3 rows rib.
Cast off loosely in rib.

## Back shoulder band

(Sizes 1, 2 and 3 only)
Work to correspond with Front Shoulder Band, omitting buttonholes. Place Front shoulder band over back shoulder band and oversew ends of bands tog at armhole edge. Sew buttons in position.

## To make up

Sizes 4 and 6 only: join left shoulder and neckband seam. Fold neckband in half onto wrong side and slip stitch loosely in position.

All sizes: Tie markers 14 (15-16-17-19) cm down from beg of shoulder shaping (or top of front shoulder band) on side edges of Back and Front to mark armholes. Sew in sleeves evenly between markers, placing centres of sleeves to shoulder seams (or top of front shoulder band). Join side and sleeve seams.

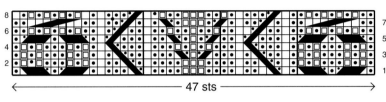

← 47 sts →

**NOTE:** Read odd numbered rows (right side rows) from right to left and even numbered rows (wrong side rows) from left to right.

### KEY

□ = Knit st on right side rows and purl st on wrong side rows.

⊡ = Purl st on right side rows and knit st on wrong side rows.

▣ = K1 tbl on right side rows and P1 tbl on wrong side rows.

▱ = Slip next st onto cable needle and leave at back of work, (K1 tbl, P1, K1 tbl) from left hand needle, then P1 from cable needle.

▰ = Slip next 3 sts onto cable needle and leave at front of work P1, then (K1 tbl, P1, K1 tbl) from cable needle.

◣ = For **right** side rows, slip next st onto cable needle and leave at front of work, P1, then K1 tbl from cable needle
For **wrong** side rows, slip next st onto cable needle and leave at front of work (side facing you), P1 tbl, then K1 from cable needle.

◢ = For **right** side rows, slip next st onto cable needle and leave at back of work, K1 tbl, then P1 from cable needle.
For **wrong** side rows, slip next st onto cable needle and leave at back of work (side facing away from you), K1, then P1 tbl from cable needle.

▱▱ = Slip next 4 sts onto cable needle and leave at back of work, (K1 tbl, P1, K1 tbl) from left hand needle, then (P1, K1 tbl) twice from cable needle.

# HAT

## Back and front

(Both alike–make 2 pieces)
Using 3.25mm needles, cast on 54 (54-58-58-58) sts.
Work 10 (10-10-12-14) cm rib as for Back of Jumper, ending with a 2nd row.
**NEXT ROW:** Rib 3 (3-8-8-5), * inc in next st, rib 2, rep from * to last 0 (0-5-5-2) sts, rib 0 (0-5-5-2). 71 (71-73-73-75) sts.
Change to 4.00mm needles and Beg Patt:
**1ST ROW (RIGHT SIDE):** K1 (1-2-2-3), (P1, K3) twice, P1, K2, work 1st row of Graph across next 47 sts, K2, P1, (K3, P1) twice, K1 (1-2-2-3).
**2ND ROW:** P12 (12-13-13-14), work 2nd row of Graph, P12 (12-13-13-14).
**3RD ROW:** K3 (3-0-0-1), (P1, K3) 2 (2-3-3-3) times, K1, work 3rd row of Graph, K1, (K3, P1) 2 (2-3-3-3) times, K3 (3-0-0-1).
**4TH ROW:** P12 (12-13-13-14), work 4th row of Graph, P12 (12-13-13-14).
**5TH ROW:** As 1st row, working 5th row of Graph.
**6TH ROW:** As 2nd row, working 6th row of Graph.
**7TH ROW:** As 3rd row, working 7th row of Graph.
**8TH ROW:** As 4th row, working 8th row of Graph.
Last 8 rows form patt.
Cont in patt until work measures 15 (16-17-18-20) cm from beg, working last row on wrong side.

SHAPE TOP
Keeping patt correct, dec one st at each end of every row until 51 (51-53-53-55) sts rem.
Cast off loosely.

## To make up

Join side and top seams, reversing seam for 5 (5-5-6-7) cm at lower edge. Fold band at lower edge in half to right side.

# Teddy's Fair Isle cardigan & scarf

## Measurements

### Cardigan

| | | |
|---|---|---|
| To fit chest (cm): | 36 | 55 |
| Actual measurement (cm): | 40 | 59 |
| Length (cm): | 13 | 18 |
| Sleeve length (cm): | 6 | 9 |

### Scarf

| | | |
|---|---|---|
| Width (cm): | 7 | 9 |
| Length (excluding fringe) (cm): | 50 | 70 |

## Materials

Cleckheaton Country 8 ply or Country Natural 8ply (50g balls)

### Cardigan

| | | |
|---|---|---|
| Main Colour (MC): | 1 | 2 |
| 1st Contrast (C1): | 1 | 1 |
| 2nd Contrast (C2): | 1 | 2 |
| 3rd Contrast (C3): | 1 | 1 |
| 4th Contrast (C4): | 1 | 1 |

### Scarf

| | | |
|---|---|---|
| Main Colour (MC): | 1 | 1 |
| 1st Contrast (C1): | 1 | 1 |
| 2nd Contrast (C2): | 1 | 1 |
| 3rd Contrast (C3): | 1 | 1 |
| 4th Contrast (C4): | 1 | 1 |

or Cleckheaton Machinewash 8 ply or Cleckheaton 8 ply Pure Wool (50g balls)

### Cardigan

| | | |
|---|---|---|
| Main Colour (MC): | 1 | 1 |
| 1st Contrast (C1): | 1 | 1 |
| 2nd Contrast (C2): | 1 | 1 |
| 3rd Contrast (C3): | 1 | 1 |
| 4th Contrast (C4): | 1 | 1 |

### Scarf

| | | |
|---|---|---|
| Main Colour (MC): | 1 | 1 |
| 1st Contrast (C1): | 1 | 1 |
| 2nd Contrast (C2): | 1 | 1 |
| 3rd Contrast (C3): | 1 | 1 |
| 4th Contrast (C4): | 1 | 1 |

One pair each 3.25mm, 4.00mm and the required size to give correct tension; knitter's needle for sewing seams; 5 small buttons for cardigan; crochet hook for scarf fringing.

## CARDIGAN

### Back

Using 3.25mm needles and MC, cast on 47 (67) sts.

**1ST ROW:** K2, * P1, K1, rep from * to last st, K1.

**2ND ROW:** K1, * P1, K1, rep from * to end.

Rep 1st and 2nd rows 1 (2) time/s, inc 4 (6) sts evenly across last row. 51 (73) sts [4 (6) rows rib in all].

Change to 4.00mm needles.

Rows 1 to 12 incl from Graph form patt. Note needle changes.

Work in patt until work measures 11.5 (16.5) cm from beg, ending with a purl row.

SHAPE BACK NECK

**NEXT ROW:** Patt 18 (25), cast off next 15 (23) sts loosely in patt, patt to end.

Keeping patt correct, cont on last 18 (25) sts and dec one st at neck edge in next 2 rows. 16 (23) sts.

## TENSION

These garments have been designed at a tension of 24 sts and 28 rows to 10cm over Fair Isle Patt, using needles as specified on Graph.

**NOTE:**

Do not weave colours in Fair Isle patt but carry colour not in use loosely across on wrong side of work. Always carry colours to ends of rows and catch in at side edge. Always carry C2 above C3 and MC, and MC above C3.

Work 1 row.
Cast off rem sts loosely in patt.
With wrong side facing, join appropriate
colour to rem 18 (25) sts.
Keeping patt correct, dec one st at neck
edge in next 2 rows.  16 (23) sts.
Work 1 row.
Cast off rem sts loosely in patt.

## Left front

Using 3.25mm needles and MC, cast on 23
(33) sts.
Work 4 (6) rows rib as given for Back, inc 2
(3) sts evenly across last row.  25 (36) sts.
Change to 4.00mm needles.
Work in patt, as indicated on Graph for
Left Front until there are 14 (22) rows less
than Back to cast-off edge, thus ending
with a purl row. **

### SHAPE FRONT SLOPE

Keeping patt correct, dec one st at end
(front edge) of next row and at same edge
in every row until 20 (31) sts rem, then in
alt rows until 16 (23) sts rem.
Work 1 row.
Cast off rem sts loosely in patt.

## Right front

Work as given for Left Front to **,
working patt from Graph as indicated for
Right Front.

### SHAPE FRONT SLOPE

Keeping patt correct, dec one st at beg
(front edge) of next row and at same edge
in every row until 20 (31) sts rem, then in
alt rows until 16 (23) sts rem.
Work 1 row.
Cast off rem sts loosely in patt.

## Sleeves

Using 3.25mm needles and MC, cast on 27
(41) sts.
Work 4 (6) rows rib as given for Back, inc 2
sts evenly across last row.  29 (43) sts.
Change to 4.00mm needles.
Work in patt from Graph as indicated for
Sleeves and noting to work extra sts into
patt, inc one st at each end of 3rd and foll
4th rows until there are 35 (51) sts.
Cont in patt (without further inc) until
work measures 6 (9) cm from beg, ending
with a purl row.
Cast off loosely in patt.

## Left front band

Join shoulder seams.  With right side
facing, using 3.25mm needles and MC,
knit up 24 (35) sts evenly from centre back
neck to beg of front slope shaping, then 25
(30) sts evenly along rem of front edge.  49
(65) sts.
Work 1 (2) row/s rib as for Back, beg with a
2nd row.
**NEXT ROW:** Rib 25 (2), [yrn, P2tog, rib 3

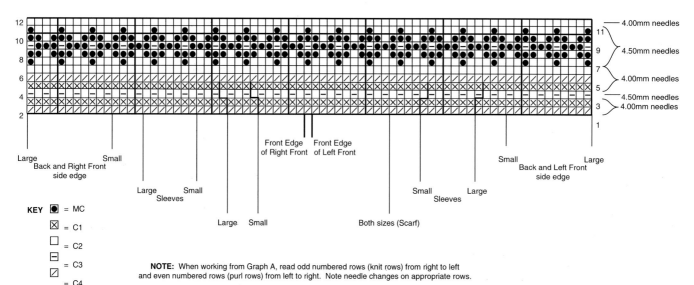

12
10
8
6
4
2

11
9
7
5
3
1

4.00mm needles
4.50mm needles
4.00mm needles
4.50mm needles
4.00mm needles

Large                          Small
Back and Right Front
side edge

Large        Small
Sleeves

Large     Small

Front Edge      Front Edge
of Right Front  of Left Front

Both sizes (Scarf)

Small      Large
Sleeves

Small              Large
Back and Left Front
side edge

**KEY**  ● = MC
☒ = C1
□ = C2
⊟ = C3
◪ = C4

**NOTE:** When working from Graph A, read odd numbered rows (knit rows) from right to left
and even numbered rows (purl rows) from left to right.  Note needle changes on appropriate rows.

**NOTE:** Not all sleeve shaping has been shown.

(4)] 4 times, yrn, P2tog, rib 2 (37).  5
buttonholes.
Work 1 (2) row/s rib.
Cast off loosely in rib.

## *Right front band*

With right side facing, using 3.25mm
needles and MC, knit up 25 (30) sts evenly
along front edge to beg of front slope
shaping, then 24 (35) sts evenly along rem
of front edge to centre of back neck.  49
(65) sts.
Work 3 (5) rows rib as for Back, beg with a
2nd row.
Cast off loosely in rib.

## *To make up*

Tie markers 7 (10) cm down from
shoulders on side edge of Back and Fronts
to mark armholes.  Sew in sleeves evenly
between markers, placing centres of
sleeves to shoulder seams.  Join side and
sleeve seams.  Join front bands at centre
back neck.  Sew on buttons.

# SCARF

Using 4.00mm needles and C4, cast on 17
(21) sts.

BEGIN PATTERN
Rows 1 to 12 incl from Graph form patt,
noting needle changes.
Work in patt until work measures approx
50 (70) cm from beg, ending with a 5th
patt row.
Using C4, cast off loosely purlways.

## *To make up*

Cut 3 lengths of MC 9 (11) cm long for
each fringe tassel.  Fold the length in half
and using the crochet hook, draw the
folded end through the edge of the knitted
fabric (working on right side).  Draw the
loose ends of the MC lengths through the
loop, then draw up securely to form a knot.
Work this fringing evenly along each end
of scarf.  Trim ends evenly.

*Messing About*

# *Striped jacket*

## TENSION

*These garments have been designed at a tension of 22 sts and 30 rows to 10cm over stocking st, using 4.00mm needles.*

## *Measurements*

| Years | | | | |
|---|---|---|---|---|
| 1 | 2 | 3 | 4 | 6 |

To fit chest (cm):

| | | | | |
|---|---|---|---|---|
| 52.5 | 55 | 57.5 | 60 | 65 |

Actual measurement (cm):

| | | | | |
|---|---|---|---|---|
| 66 | 72 | 77 | 82 | 90 |

Length (approx) (cm):

| | | | | |
|---|---|---|---|---|
| 39 | 42 | 44 | 47 | 51 |

Sleeve length (cm):

| | | | | |
|---|---|---|---|---|
| 19 | 21 | 23 | 26 | 31 |

## *Materials*

Cleckheaton Country 8 ply or Country Naturals 8 ply or Cleckheaton Machinewash 8 ply or Cleckheaton 8 ply Pure Wool (50g balls)

Jacket with hood

1st Contrast (C1):

| | | | | |
|---|---|---|---|---|
| 2 | 2 | 2 | 3 | 3 |

2nd Contrast (C2):

| | | | | |
|---|---|---|---|---|
| 2 | 2 | 2 | 3 | 3 |

3rd Contrast (C3):

| | | | | |
|---|---|---|---|---|
| 2 | 2 | 2 | 2 | 3 |

4th Contrast (C4):

| | | | | |
|---|---|---|---|---|
| 1 | 1 | 1 | 2 | 2 |

5th Contrast (C5):

| | | | | |
|---|---|---|---|---|
| 2 | 2 | 2 | 3 | 3 |

Jacket without hood

1st Contrast (C1):

| | | | | |
|---|---|---|---|---|
| 2 | 2 | 2 | 3 | 3 |

2nd Contrast (C2):

| | | | | |
|---|---|---|---|---|
| 1 | 1 | 2 | 2 | 2 |

3rd Contrast (C3):

| | | | | |
|---|---|---|---|---|
| 1 | 1 | 2 | 2 | 2 |

4th Contrast (C4):

| | | | | |
|---|---|---|---|---|
| 1 | 1 | 1 | 1 | 2 |

5th Contrast (C5):

| | | | | |
|---|---|---|---|---|
| 1 | 1 | 2 | 2 | 2 |

One pair 4.00mm knitting needles or the required size to give correct tension; 1 stitch holder for Jacket Without Hood; knitter's needle for sewing seams and embroidery; 8 (9-9-10-10) buttons.

## JACKET WITH HOOD

### *Back*

Using 4.00mm needles and C5, cast on 75 (81-87-93-101) sts.

Work 116 (122-130-136-148) rows stocking st, in stripes of 12 (12-14-14-16) rows C5, 12 (12-14-14-16) rows C1, 8 (8-10-10-10) rows C2, 12 rows C3, 8 (8-8-8-10) rows C4, 10 (10-10-12-12) rows C5, 12 (12-14-14-16) rows C2, 8 (8-10-10-10) rows C3, 12 rows C1, 8 (8-8-8-10) rows C5, 10 (12-10-12-12) rows C4 and 4 (8-8-10-12) rows C1.

SHAPE SHOULDERS

Using C1 for rem, cast off 6 (7-7-8-9) sts at beg of next 6 rows, then 7 (6-9-9-9) sts at beg of foll 2 rows.

Cast off rem 25 (27-27-27-29) sts loosely.

### *Left front*

(If making for girl, omit buttonholes)

Using 4.00mm needles and C5, cast on 38 (41-44-47-51) sts.

Work 107 (111-119-123-135) rows stocking st in stripes as given for Back, at same time working a buttonhole in 5th (5th-5th-3rd-5th) row and foll 14th (13th-14th-13th-14th) rows, noting to work buttonholes along front edge as folls:

ON RIGHT SIDE ROWS: Knit to last 4 sts, yfwd, K2tog, K2, or

ON WRONG SIDE ROWS: P2, P2tog, yrn, purl to end.

There will be 8 (9-9-10-10) buttonholes
worked in all.

SHAPE NECK
Keeping stripes correct, cast off 6 sts at beg
of next row.  32 (35-38-41-45) sts.
Dec one st at neck edge in every row until
27 (30-33-38-40) sts rem, then in alt row/s
until 26 (28-31-34-37) sts rem.
Work 1 row.

SHAPE SHOULDER
Cast off 6 (7-7-8-9) sts at beg of next and
foll alt rows 3 times in all, at same time dec
one st at neck edge in first row.
Work 1 row.  Cast off rem 7 (6-9-9-9) sts.

## Right front
(If making for boy, omit buttonholes)
Using 4.00mm needles and C5, cast on 38
(41-44-47-51) sts.
Work 106 (110-118-122-134) rows stocking
st in stripes as given for Back, at same time
working a buttonhole in 5th (5th-3rd-3rd-
5th) row and foll 14th (13th-14th-13th-
14th) rows, noting to work buttonholes
along front edge as folls:
**ON RIGHT SIDE ROWS:** K2, K2tog, yfwd,
knit to end, or
**ON WRONG SIDE ROWS:** Purl to last 4 sts,
yrn, P2tog, P2.
There will be 8 (9-9-10-10) buttonholes
worked in all.

SHAPE NECK
Keeping stripes correct, cast off 6 sts at beg
of next row.  32 (35-38-41-45) sts.
Work 1 row.
Dec one st at neck edge in every row until
27 (30-33-38-40) sts rem, then in alt row/s
until 25 (27-30-33-36) sts rem.

SHAPE SHOULDER
Cast off 6 (7-7-8-9) sts at beg of next and
alt rows 3 times in all.
Work 1 row.  Cast off rem 7 (6-9-9-9) sts.

## Sleeves
Using 4.00mm needles and C1, cast on 43
(45-45-47-49) sts.
Work throughout in stocking st stripes as
given for Back, [omitting first C5 stripe
and beg with 12 (12-14-14-16) rows C1] at

same time inc one st at each end of 3rd
and foll alt (3rd-alt-3rd-3rd) row/s until
there are 47 (67-61-89-83) sts, then in foll
3rd (4th-3rd-4th-4th) row/s until there are
75 (77-89-91-99) sts.
Cont in stripes (without further inc) until
work measures 19 (21-23-26-31) cm from
beg, ending with a purl row.

SHAPE TOP
Cast off 6 (6-7-7-8) sts at beg of next 8
rows, then 6 (6-8-8-8) sts at beg of foll 2
rows.
Cast off rem 15 (17-17-19-19) sts.

## Hood
Using 4.00mm needles and C1, cast on 37
(39-41-43-45) sts.
Work 70 (72-74-76-78) rows stocking st in
stripes as given for Back [omitting first C5
stripe and beg with 12 (12-14-14-16) rows
C1].

SHAPE TOP
Keeping stripes correct, dec one st at end
of next and alt rows until 31 (33-35-37-39)
sts rem, then at same edge in every row
until 27 (29-31-33-35) sts rem.
Work 1 row, thus ending with a purl row
and 4 (6-12-12-8) rows of C5 (C5-C1-C1-
C1).
Working stripes in reverse from this point
[i.e. work 4 (6-12-12-8) rows C5 (C5-C1-
C1-C1), then 12 (12-10-10-10) rows C1
(C1-C3-C3-C3) etc], inc one st at beg of
2nd row and at same edge in every row
until there are 32 (34-36-38-40) sts, then in
alt rows until there are 37 (39-41-43-45)
sts.
Cont working stripes in reverse and work
70 (72-74-76-78) rows stocking st, thus
ending with 12 (12-14-14-16) rows C1.
Cast off.

## Edgings

SLEEVE EDGING
With right side facing, using 4.00mm
needles and C1, knit up 41 (43-43-45-47)
sts evenly around lower sleeve edge.
Knit 1 row.
Cast off loosely knitways.

LOWER EDGING

Join side seams for Back and Fronts for
10cm from lower edge.  With right side
facing, using 4.00mm needles and C5, knit
up 147 (159-171-183-199) sts evenly
around lower edge of Back and Fronts.
Complete as for Sleeve Edging.

LEFT FRONT EDGING

With right side facing, using 4.00mm
needles and C5, knit up 75 (81-85-91-99)
sts evenly along left front edge.
Complete as given for Sleeve Edging.

RIGHT FRONT EDGING

Work to correspond with Left Front
Edging.

HOOD EDGING

With right side facing, using 4.00mm
needles and C5, knit up 127 (129-133-135-
139) sts evenly along straight edge of hood.
Complete as given for Sleeve Edging.

## To make up

Using Knitting St, embroider circles from
Graph to Jacket, using C5 on 12 row C3
stripe and C4 on 12 row C1 stripe, as
illustrated.  Tie markers 16 (17-19-20-22)
cm down from beg of shoulder shaping on
side edges of Back and Fronts to mark
armholes.  Join shoulder seams.  Sew in
sleeves evenly between markers, placing
centres of sleeves to shoulder seams.  Join
rem of side and sleeve seams, carefully
matching stripes.
Fold hood in half and join back shaped
seam, carefully matching stripes.  Attach to
neck edge, beg and ending at centre fronts
and gathering extra fullness across back
neck.
Using C1  double, work Blanket St evenly
along  lower, front, sleeves and hood
edges.  Sew on buttons.

## JACKET WITHOUT HOOD

Work Back, Left Front, Right Front,
Sleeves, Sleeve Edging and Lower Edging
as for Jacket with Hood, noting to leave
Back neck sts on stitch holder instead of
casting-off.

## Neckband

Join shoulder seams.  With right side
facing, using 3.25mm needles and C5, knit
up 69 (75-75-79-81) sts evenly around
neck, incl sts from stitch holder.
Knit 1 row.
Cast off loosely.

## Left front edging

With right side facing, using 4.00mm
needles and C5, knit up 83 (89-93-99-107)
sts evenly along left front edge and end of

neckband.
Complete as given for Sleeve Edging of Jacket with Hood.

## Right front edging

Work to correspond with Left Front Edging.

## To make up

Using Knitting St, embroider circles from Graph to Jacket, using C5 on 12 row C3 stripe and C4 on 12 row C1 stripe, as illustrated. Tie markers 16 (17-19-20-22) cm down from beg of shoulder shaping on side edges of Back and Fronts to mark armholes. Sew in sleeves evenly between markers, placing centres of sleeves to shoulder seams. Join rem of side and sleeve seams, carefully matching stripes. Using C1 double, work Blanket St evenly along lower, front, neck and sleeves edges. Sew on buttons.

*Aran jumper & hat (page 67); Teddy's waistcoat (page 46); Striped jacket with and without hood (page 76).*

*Shirt, bandana, duffle jacket, pants and pinafores from Osh Kosh B'Gosh. Skivvies from Homegrown. Teddies from The Teddy Bear Shop.*

**PROJECT MANAGER:**
Kate Tully

**STYLIST:**
Louise Owens

**PHOTOGRAPHER:**
Andrew Elton

**MAKE-UP:**
Julie Elton

Special thanks to our models: Anthony, Cassandra, Kristy, Lana, Natasha, Paige, Patrick and Wesley.

**DESIGNS CREATED AND KNITTED BY**
Australian Country Spinners Pty Ltd
314 – 320 Albert Street
Brunswick, Victoria 3056
Telephone (03) 380 3888 (for all queries)

All contact details were correct at time of printing.

A Bay Books Publication

Bay Books, an imprint of
HarperCollins Publishers
25 Ryde Road, Pymble, Sydney NSW 2073, Australia
31 View Road, Glenfield, Auckland 10, New Zealand

First published in Australia in 1994

Designs copyright © Australian Country Spinners 1994
This book copyright © Bay Books 1994

This book is copyright.
Apart from any fair dealing for the purposes of private study,
research, criticism or review, as permitted under the Copyright Act,
no part may be reproduced by any process without written
permission. Inquiries should be addressed to the publishers.

National Library of Australia
Cataloguing-in-Publication data:

Knits for kids and teddies, too.

ISBN 1 86378 145 5.

   1. Knitting - Patterns. 2. Children's clothing - Patterns. 3. Teddy bears.
   I. Australian Country Spinners.

746.92
Printed in Singapore
9 8 7 6 5 4 3 2 1
97 96 95 94

**STOCKISTS**

Charlton Horseland
For your nearest store phone (02) 419 5900

Hide 'n Seek
611 Military Road
Mosman NSW 2088
Ph: (02) 960 1039

Julia Walton
22 Maranoa Street
Wyoming NSW 2250
Ph: (043) 29 1588

Linen and Lace of Balmain
213 Darling Street
Balmain NSW 2041
Ph: (02) 810 0719

Osh Kosh B'Gosh
for your nearest store phone (02) 699 8244

Homegrown
35 Bay Street
Double Bay NSW 2028
Ph: (02) 362 4362

Shoes & Sox
For your nearest stockist phone (02) 906 5743

Teddy & Friends
Lower Ground Floor
124a Chatswood Chase
Ph: (02) 413 1780
Head office phone: (02) 660 3577

The Teddy Bear Shop
162 Military Road
Neutral Bay NSW 2089
Ph: (02) 953 3394

Thomas Cook Boot and Clothing Co.
790 George Street
Haymarket NSW 2000
Ph: (02) 212 6616